THE AUTOBIOGRAPHY OF
ELDER HELVÉCIO MARTINS

THE AUTOBIOGRAPHY OF
ELDER HELVÉCIO MARTINS

HELVÉCIO MARTINS

WITH

MARK GROVER

The Autobiography of Elder Helvécio Martins
Copyright 1994 by Helvécio Martins
All rights reserved

No portion of this book may be reproduced in any form without written permission from the publisher, Aspen Books, 6211 South 380 West, Salt Lake City, UT 84107.

Library of Congress Cataloging-in-Publication Data
Martins, Helvécio, 1930–
  The autobiography of Elder Helvécio Martins / by Helvécio Martins; translated by Mark Grover.
      p.   cm.
  ISBN 1-56236-218-6
  1. Martins, Helvécio, 1930– . 2. Mormons—Brazil—Biography. 3. Mormon Church—Brazil—Biography. 4. Church of Jesus Christ of Latter-Day Saints—Brazil—Biography.   Title.
BX8695.M33A3   1994
289.3'092—dc20
[B]   94-37044
                                                                        CIP

Printed in the United States of America

5 4 3 2 1

Cover design by Ron Stucki
Cover photo ©The Church of Jesus Christ of Latter-day Saints. Used by permission.
Map on page 34 created by Thomas Child

CONTENTS

PREFACE	vii
THE CALL	1
MY YOUTH	4
RUDÁ	19
THE SHALLOWNESS OF SUCCESS	26
CONVERSION	39
THE PRIESTHOOD	61
TRIALS AND BLESSINGS	74
FORTALEZA	95
SERVANT OF THE LORD	110
EPILOGUE	128

PREFACE

For several years, friends have suggested that the story of our lives and the circumstances surrounding our conversion and growth in the gospel would be of value and interest to the members of the Church. I have resisted writing about my experiences because I do not perceive them to be significantly different from those of most members. I questioned whether the experiences of an average member of the Church such as myself would be of interest to those who have confronted similar challenges.

We have all made covenants to defend the kingdom of God and use all of our force and energy to help establish Zion. I rejoice when I see members successfully overcoming the challenges of this life. I observe with great sadness failures resulting from a lack of commitment to the gospel. I struggle as I see friends unable to surmount the difficulties of this life, while if they could, this would result in their receiving the joy and happiness that comes from living the commandments. If the story of my life, as uneventful as it is, can be a help to members of the Church, then I am willing to tell it. With this in mind, when a formal invitation came from Aspen Books to write my history and experiences in the Church, I accepted the invitation. It is not with egoism or pride that I write this story, but with the desire that it might serve a positive function in the establishment of the kingdom of God on this earth. If this were to happen I would be pleased.

Most of the work on this book was done in August of 1991 when I was physically incapacitated by a serious neck and back injury, so it did not interfere with my duties as a member of the Brazil Area Presidency.

I thank our Father in Heaven for life itself and for our Savior Jesus Christ, who, through his atoning sacrifice, is the author of our eternal salvation. I am grateful for help to resist the evil and lies of the world and the ability to preserve our hearts, souls, and minds free from the influences of the world. I thank the Lord for having placed in my path worthy, faithful, and dedicated men and women, who instructed and oriented my family in such a way that we were able to remain on the correct path. Of these, I am particularly grateful for my father and mother. They were good and humble people who, though they had limited schooling, were blessed with strong and righteous characters. Their standards of honesty and integrity were the same as those of the kingdom of God. They were chosen to be my parents and to teach me values and virtues that would enable me to accept and understand the gospel of Jesus Christ.

PREFACE

I give thanks for the life of a wonderful woman, my wife, Rudá. Her example of virtue, honesty, and love cannot be equaled. She is a valiant and powerful instrument in the hands of the Lord and has never wavered in her support, help, love, and motivation for me. She has been a mother and wife of unequal talent and ability. I cannot imagine life without her.

I thank the faithful members of the Church in all parts of the world, but especially from Brazil, who have been an influence on me. Their help, enthusiasm, and confidence have been immeasurable. I extend thanks and honor to the missionaries who brought us the gospel. I am grateful for the influence of the local leaders of my first branch and district and all other areas of the Church where I have lived. I thank the General Authorities whom we have met from our first years in the Church to the present. They are men of powerful and spiritual strength.

I single out President Spencer W. Kimball, whom we were privileged to first meet in Rio de Janeiro when he was president of the Quorum of Twelve Apostles. Full of affection, love, and thoughtfulness, he was a powerful influence for good in our lives. President Kimball always had time to give counsel and motivation. I consider it one of the greatest privileges of my life to have known this man.

I give thanks to Mark L. Grover, a dedicated and faithful servant of Jesus Christ. He has spent much of his life serving the Brazilian people with whom he worked as a missionary. It was his diligence as a translator and editor that resulted in the completion of this book. I have complete confidence in him, respect, and admiration for his gifts and talents. I consider him a dear friend. I also give thanks to Nuno Pereira and Russell Robe who helped in the translation and editing.

I also thank Curtis Taylor, Stan Zenk, and the staff of Aspen Books. Their interest in this project and work towards its fruition are greatly appreciated. Likewise, Elizabeth Vandenburghe's editing expertise and efforts helped make this book possible.

I offer this record and history of my life with respect and love to all who are valiantly confronting the challenges of mortal life and have hope of receiving rest and peace in the kingdom of God. I pray that the things recorded in this small book can strengthen your confidence in the Lord. It is my desire that you know that he is the father of our spirits, the provider of life, the helper in our battles, and the one most interested that we overcome the difficulties of this life. So great was his love for us that he gave his only begotten son to save our souls. We must have confidence in our Savior, the father of our salvation and Redeemer of our lives.

We are not alone; the Lord provides for us, speaks to us, and guides us through his living prophets. The Church of Jesus Christ of Latter-day Saints is his church and kingdom here on the earth. We come unto Christ by receiving the ordinances of the gospel from those who have been called by prophecy and revelation. We must continue to strive with all our hearts, might, mind, and strength through prayer, fasting, and enduring to the end. If we do all of this we will gain exaltation in his kingdom. I pray that together we can act with complete devotion, faith, and confidence in the Lord. It is with total and profound love in my heart that I pray that all can have God's eternal blessings.

Elder Helvécio Martins

©The Church of Jesus Christ of Latter-day Saints. Used by permission.

THE CALL

Sleep would not come as I lay awake in a Salt Lake City hotel room on what seemed the longest night of my life. Earlier that day, March 29, 1990, I had met with President Thomas S. Monson, who extended a call to me to become a member of the Second Quorum of the Seventy of The Church of Jesus Christ of Latter-day Saints. Rudá, my wife, and I were shocked. Only one week earlier, we had received an unusual invitation to attend general conference in Salt Lake City—unusual especially because I was busily serving as a mission president in Fortaleza, Brazil. No reason accompanied our invitation, and we didn't know what to expect.

Our expectations, frankly, never included becoming leaders in the Church, not then, and not when we had joined many years before. Back then, as black Latter-day Saints, we didn't expect to enjoy the blessings of holding the priesthood or of attending the temple. We simply wanted to serve in the Church we knew to be true even during our initial visit with the missionaries. While the 1978 revelation granting the priesthood to all worthy male members meant a great deal to us and to our family, even that immense blessing wasn't necessary for us to remain in the Church. Joining it had given us not only the truth, but also blessings Rudá and I had never before known.

I grew up in a small home near the then-Brazilian capital of Rio de Janeiro. My parents, though hard-working and faithful people, struggled to raise seven children in poverty. With great sadness I left school at twelve in order to work and help support the family. It was years later, with Rudá's encouragement, before I returned to the classroom. This began what would be many years of working a full-time job by day and attending school by night. I worked hard to obtain an education, trying to prepare for a career that would allow me to adequately raise a family.

Scenes from my past kept intruding on my sleep as I lay awake that night after meeting with President Monson. My life, granted, had been filled with challenges. But were my challenges significantly different from those of other members? No. The financial struggles coexisted alongside a fulfilling professional life and a rich family life, one that included a wonderful companion who was an excellent wife and mother. Blessings, hardships—my life didn't differ from others within the Church. Certainly, nothing in my experience had adequately prepared me for a position in the Quorum of the Seventy.

I prayed and pondered through most of the night, gradually coming to an acceptance of the overwhelming calling that had come to me. Not that I actually felt worthy of the position, but I did realize the Lord would help me, as he always helps those who try to serve him. Relief only arrived when I thought on this help, and anticipated one more call to work for the establishment of the Kingdom of God on the earth.

MY YOUTH

I was born on July 27, 1930, the oldest child of Honório and Benedita Martins. Descendants of African slaves, my parents had no written ancestral records. Along with the abolition of slavery in Brazil in 1888 came the destruction of most slave family files. I hope to one day discover something that will help me identify my ancestors, but for now, I know only that they came to Brazil as part of the three million Africans brought between 1550 and 1850 for plantation and mine work. I assume that my forebears disembarked where all slaves in the region ended their journey, Rio de Janeiro. From there, it was on to coastal area plantations near cities like Angra dos Reis, Mangaratiba, Paratí, and Manbucaba.

My parents married on July 24, 1929, and I came one year later. Eventually, they had six more children: my sisters Ivete, Ivonete, Ivani, and Iri, and my brothers Honório and Jorge. My father and mother lived humbly most of their lives, but passed on valuable lessons of faith, love, honor, and justice to their children. I revere them the way Nephi honored his parents when he began the Book of Mormon: "I, Nephi, having been born of goodly parents, therefore I was taught somewhat in all the learning of my father; and having seen many afflictions in the course of my days, nevertheless, having been highly favored of the Lord in all my days; yea, having had a great knowledge of the goodness and the mysteries of God, therefore I make a record of my proceedings in my days" (1 Ne. 1:1).

My father was tall and strong compared to most Brazilians. A strong character accompanied his physical prowess, one that could not tolerate dishonesty, injustice, or inequality. Although he was unable to read, Father resolved disagreements with integrity and intelligence, and I witnessed many such conflicts as a child. Sometimes he handled the disagreement with amiability and words, other times with anger and physical force.

One incident in particular illustrates well his use of the latter method. Father was defending what he considered his primary responsibility—his family. My mother had injured her shoulder while Father was at work, but came home from the hospital with only a splint and no proper treatment. When Father discovered that the hospital had informed Mother that the doctors would not fix her shoulder that day, but that she should return the next day, he rushed her back to the emergency room immediately.

"This is a crime!" he cried to the attendant, who again informed my mother she would have to return the next day. "You can't stay like this until tomorrow," Father explained to Mother, and went on to inform the hospital staff that he wasn't asking for a special favor. He paid for insurance which went to the hospital each month, he insisted, and thus his family was entitled to receive medical care when they needed it. Father kept insisting. The staff kept resisting. After a while, my father picked up a chair and began breaking everything in sight. Several men rushed to subdue him, but considering my father's strength, not to mention the chair he wielded, he easily knocked them down and managed to destroy much of the room.

I cannot judge my father too harshly, especially since his actions resulted in my mother's proper and immediate medical treatment that day. He cared deeply for his family to the point that he spent his entire life at hard labor trying to sustain them. From him, I learned to work hard and, even more important, to put my faith in God and abhor dishonesty, injustice, and inequality.

We lived in the city of Rio de Janeiro, renowned for its long white beaches outlining the vibrant blue of the Atlantic Ocean. Just beyond the coast, stunning mountains of black volcanic rock jut through lush vegetation, surrounding a colorful city that moves to a samba rhythm. Above it all, the *Corcovado*, one of the world's most famous statues of Christ, overlooks the incredible combination of natural and manmade beauty that is Rio de Janeiro.

The *Corcovado* overlooking Rio de Janeiro.

I grew up, like many residents of Rio, appreciative both of my city's striking beauty and of its importance to Brazil. Located on the country's southeastern seaboard, Rio de Janeiro is the entry port for much of Brazil's shipping. Once home to the King of Portugal in the early 1800s, Rio became the seat of government for the new independent country of Brazil in 1822. It served as Brazil's capital until 1960, when Brasilia, newly constructed in the country's less-populated interior, took over the responsibility.

The rural part of Rio, called Santa Cruz, was my childhood home, an area typical of south central Brazil in its mix of cultures and traditions. Agriculturally prosperous, the region's oranges, sugarcane, sweet potatoes, and various other fruits and vegetables flourished under the hot sun and warm rains. Modest cattle farms supplied meat to the city, and a large number of immigrants offered an array of services. Syrian, Lebanese, and Turkish businessmen ran the stores. Italians baked breads and pastries, and marketed textiles and grain. A few Portuguese and Spanish immigrants were numbered among us as well. During the 1940s, Japanese families settled in government-established agricultural colonies and introduced new farming techniques that greatly improved crop yields.

My family prospered in this region until my early childhood. Father bought hides from the local butchers and made an excellent living selling them. He conducted his business around our kitchen table, and his work provided an abundance and variety of food. He also hired nannies for the children, one assigned to care for each child. Unfortunately, this time of prosperity for us ended, never to return.

My family's grave financial difficulties first began in the mid-1930s, when changes in government policies seriously hurt my father's business. An idealist and dreamer, Father always expected our situation to improve, believing that life would someday be as prosperous as it had been. But the more he dreamed, the worse our condition became.

The first hint I had of our financial predicament came with the Christmas I discovered the truth about Santa Claus. I was about six years old, and according to neighborhood tradition, I should have received the toy truck I asked Santa for in the empty shoe I had set out on the window sill. But I woke up on Christmas morning to find, much to my dismay, nothing in the shoe. I checked my younger brother's shoe and was even more disturbed to find it empty as well. Maybe, I hoped, Santa Claus was late. Yet when I went into our backyard, children on both sides of our house sat playing with new Christmas toys. With the innocence of a six-year-old, I believed a great injustice had occurred, until my mother painfully explained that our family had no money for presents that year.

I have a special place in my heart for my parents, having watched them struggle through that difficult period.

My father worked constantly, and at times irritability replaced some of his good humor. He went from owning his own business, and the economic comforts it entailed, to working for the mayor's office for minimal pay. On top of that, his paycheck often arrived late, as the mayor's funds for the district remained at the discretion of President Getúlio Vargas, who often disagreed with the mayor's policies and consequently withheld funds.

To make up for his small and often unreliable salary, Father arranged a second job in the evening manually demolishing buildings. President Vargas, in spite of his human failings, prudently envisioned the need for ample traffic routes in the burgeoning city of Rio. Without the help of mechanical equipment like bulldozers, men like my father used sledgehammers and hand-held tools to tear down existing buildings between several old streets to create a large avenue. My father would leave his government job in the late afternoon, return home to change and eat a little, then go to the town's center to demolish buildings.

Work doesn't ordinarily kill a person, but this backbreaking labor combined with my father's other intense efforts to support our family, I'm sure, hastened the onset of his ill health and death in later years. I remember seeing my father get up at six in the morning and stand under a cement water tank adjacent to our house where he let a strong stream of water loose on his head. He said that water was the only thing that could wake him up.

Before leaving in the morning, he ate very little. Food for his children, he felt, should be first priority. He didn't return home from his second job until early in the morning. He then often slept sitting up in a chair, afraid that if he lay down, he would not be able to get up the next day.

I seldom saw my father in those years, but never stopped loving him. My courageous mother tried to ease his financial burden by doing what she could to help. After learning to make the braided-straw furniture popular back then, she and my father produced chairs for extra money. And later, my mother informed me after his death, my father accepted a government offer of early retirement with full salary. This may have been the only moment of weakness in my father's life, for the offer came from the commission designated to investigate the hospital incident in which my angry father tore apart the room.

The commission concluded that my father's rage was justified; however, they felt that a favorable ruling for my father would tarnish the image of government officials like themselves. So, using the incentive of this early retirement arrangement, they asked my father to declare himself mentally unstable. With this, the case would be closed, nobody would be blamed, and my father could receive his city paycheck along with time to work elsewhere for additional money. He accepted the proposal. My mother, assigned as his guardian, received his check, and Father then worked at other jobs. Again, I cannot judge my father too harshly; his concern for his family came before his health, well-being, and even personal pride.

I, too, tried to help out our family's situation by attending school in the morning and spending the rest of the day doing odd jobs—weeding gardens, cleaning orange groves, working as much as possible. But although manual labor consumed a disproportionate amount of my childhood, my early years in school influenced my life in countless ways, some negative, some positive.

I attended two elementary schools (*primária*), the first of which—a small, disorganized classroom in a house—I remember very little about. I then transferred to a new school after going to live with my maternal grandmother to ease my family's situation. *Nossa Senhora da Conceição* (Our Lady of the Conception), owned by a faithful Catholic woman and her equally faithful son, was big and spacious, situated on a large lot. Students could eat fruit from the many trees in the school yard, but that liberty constituted almost the only freedom we were allowed at the institution.

When I enrolled in Nossa Senhora, my grandfather said to the principal, "Treat him the way you would treat your own son." The principal found me a good student and consequently befriended me, for I was so terrified by the school that I studied very hard, memorizing entire pages (which I can still recall) to avoid punishment. The curriculum included obligatory religious instruction, such as the Catholic catechism, as well as regular school

MY YOUTH

subjects. Those unable to recite their catechism, special prayers, or other lessons received no recess. Students who lagged in their studies received physical punishments, which included standing or kneeling in a corner while facing the wall for hours at a time. Instructors also used paddles and rulers to reprimand and humiliate.

Unfortunately, parents in those days accepted and encouraged this type of physical punishment. I felt, and I still feel, that such methods are anti-educational and degrading, detrimental to the learning process in their way of teaching through fear. Although considered a good student by the administrators, I was, in reality, only a terrified student. The fear of punishment, much more than a love of learning, motivated me to study for hours on end.

After elementary school, I passed an entrance exam and was admitted to the most prestigious junior high school (*ginásio*) in the region, Belisário do Santos. Owned by a well-known lawyer who also served as its principal, the school was in Campo Grande, about twelve to fifteen miles from my home in Santa Cruz. I traveled daily from Santa Cruz to Campo Grande on a slow train pulled by a wood-burning steam engine and didn't mind the commute, for I liked the school and learned a great deal during my short stay there.

The students met together early in the morning, sang the national anthem, then separated into different classes. My teachers were excellent, particularly Mr. Filho, who taught Portuguese and Latin, and Mr. Murilo, my history teacher. But the teacher I remember most was Mr. Jair, who taught mathematics. With a strong intellect and adept teaching ability, he motivated us to learn and made it easy and interesting with his relaxed manner.

Mr. Jair also taught me more than mathematics. I learned a lesson in his class about keeping away from bad influences that I never forgot. When I began the school year, I sat close to a group of rowdy students who, one day, made me laugh at one of their antics. Mr. Jair turned around from the blackboard and said, "Helvécio, I am disappointed in you. Leave the classroom." Following the rules for dismissed students, I stayed in the hall waiting for the class to end, wandering from one side to the other. Soon the principal appeared.

An imposing man with an authoritative air, he queried, "What is your name?"

"Helvécio Martins," I replied.

"What are you doing in the hall?" he asked. Humiliated, I explained I had been dismissed from class. Then he declared, "You must not be a very good student if this happened to you." I wanted to hide my face in shame, to run and find a good place to cry. Right then, I made a vow that this experience would never happen again, and it never did. From then on, I sat on the front row of the classroom and away from that group of boys. Even when I returned to school as an adult, I always sat on the front row, never in the middle.

Unfortunately, much as I enjoyed my brief stay in junior high school, the experience ended up being just that: brief. My family's lack of funds required not only my leaving school at age eleven, but also my search for full-time work. I found it picking oranges in the many groves of Rio de Janeiro, one of the largest orange-producing regions in the country.

Early in the morning, a truck would stop at a designated area to pick up workers and take them to the orange groves. There I was, a young boy just under twelve, waiting at 4:00 or 5:00 in the morning to go to work with boys and men much older than I was. Even so, work gave me good experiences and doubtless aided in my personal development. In my youthful innocence, I enjoyed the work, and especially the money I earned to help my parents. Because we received pay not by the hour, but by the number of oranges we picked, I worked long hours, returning home at night very tired. Later, at age thirteen, I began working with the National Health Service, digging and clearing out vegetation in ditches in areas without natural drainage.

When my father began working for the city, my family moved from Santa Cruz to an area closer to downtown Rio called Irajá. I decided to join my family there after realizing better-paying jobs existed in the city, and sadly left the grandfather who had treated me so well. With the help of friends, I secured a job in downtown Rio on Silva Jardim Street, taking messages and mail around the city. I had assured the owner, Mr. Pedroso, of my familiarity with the city when, in reality, I knew nothing about Rio de Janeiro. I have since repented of that lie, but at the time I needed a job very badly. Fortunately, Rio is an easy city to master, and I learned the city's layout within days.

Later, Mr. Pedroso sold the business, and the two buyers, whom I had known for years, took over and kept me on while they shifted the business to law and bookkeeping. From their office near São Francisco Plaza, they worked with large and important companies as well as small businesses. I worked hard for them. They liked and trusted me.

My work consumed my time in Irajá, but politics consumed the minds and made up the worries of everyone in Brazil during that period and beyond. Shortly after my family moved to Rio, World War II broke out. I remember gathering firewood with a friend one day and returning to completely empty streets at three in the afternoon. Everyone was inside listening to President Vargas announce Brazil's declaration of war on the Axis countries of Germany and Italy. When the president concluded, people ran into the streets crying. A distant war had suddenly become very personal. Brazil participated in several facets of the war, including sending troops to fight in Italy. On a particularly sad day, friends in our neighborhood left for Europe as part of the first Brazilian contingent to fight there.

MY YOUTH

Because our neighborhood was poor, few of us owned radios, so we frequently gathered together in the homes of the handful who did. The government-run "Rádio Nacional" began its news spots with a drumroll and bugles playing, after which the somber voice of Eron Domingues began the report. I will never forget the day he announced the war's end. Joyful celebration erupted everywhere, especially when the Brazilian Expeditionary Forces arrived home from Italy. After disembarking near Rio de Jeneiro, the soldiers marched single file down both sides of Rio's main street, Central Avenue, dressed in their uniforms and still carrying their backpacks. Masses of people filled the street, trying to touch the soldiers, hugging each other, cheering, weeping. I will never forget that scene.

The war ended, but Brazil's political turmoil continued. In 1945, a bloodless military coup ousted our own dictatorship, for how could Brazil justify sending troops to fight fascism in Europe while simultaneously preserving a similar system at home? Thus, President Getúlio Vargas, who had governed Brazil for fifteen years, was replaced by a provisional government until presidential elections could take place the following year. Brazil's congress (*Câmara dos Deputados*), which had not been functioning, now reconvened.

These promising events, unfortunately, were not the prelude to democracy everyone hoped for. Vargas still possessed incredible influence. While still in power, he organized two strong political parties (made up of the elites and the lower classes, respectively) whose candidate, Eurico Gaspar Dutra, Vargas's former minister of war, won the election. In a successive election four years later, Vargas ran for president against Brigadier General Eduardo Gomes of the Democratic Union Party. Using deception and misinformation, Vargas twisted the meaning of Gomes's platforms, making him appear elitist and unwilling to associate with the workers.

Getúlio Vargas thus won the election in 1950 and again became Brazil's president, this time democratically elected. But his administration, racked with charges of corruption, abuse, and dishonesty, floundered under immense economic and social pressures. On the morning of August 24, 1954, I was climbing the stairs on my way to work and heard the drumroll of the radio news. The voice of Eron Domingues solemnly announced that President Vargas had shot himself in the chest.

My potentially productive country, so rich in human and natural resources, has been plagued with political tragedies such as these since the 1930s. Innumerable government strategies for transforming our problems have only served to stifle our progress. Some good programs have emerged, granted, but ever since my youth, I have seen Brazil, my country, suffer from one tragedy after another.

RUDÁ

In 1953 our office needed to hire a new clerk and advertised the opening through the Ministry of Labor's job service. One day shortly thereafter, a young woman came in for an interview and I heard her voice in the room next to mine. The sound of it attracted me and I listened to the entire interview through the wall. After my boss offered her the job and instructed her to return the next day, I rushed out of my office and into the reception area, hoping to see the woman's face. All that I saw was her profile, but the image had an extraordinary effect on me. I waited anxiously for the next day to arrive.

When I came to work the following day, Rudá Tourinho Assis was already there, the most beautiful woman I had ever seen. I loved her from the moment I first saw her and immediately lost interest in the girl I was dating at the time. Determined to win Rudá over, I did everything in my power to make a good impression, even calling her once, at the risk of being overheard, while in the home of my old girlfriend.

Finally, I mustered enough courage to ask Rudá out, and on June 18, 1953, we had our first date, a movie. After I took her home and we said our good-byes, I did something I still can't believe I had the audacity to even think of. I asked her to marry me. Of course, she said no. How could she have said anything else on our first date, before we even knew each other? And how could I have gotten married, anyway, while still helping to support my father's family? My only rationale for that daring proposal lies in the fact that I knew what I wanted and she was it. I felt as though I had known her for years and still romantically compare our relationship to that of Jimmy Stewart and his wife in *It's a Wonderful Life*: We were destined to meet, perhaps in the premortal life.

Although Rudá didn't accept my hasty offer of marriage, she continued to see me and encouraged me to return to school and finish my education. She knew well the benefits of financial stability, for her father worked for the city courts, where I had seen him while on my errands for my company. I knew he was a financially prosperous man with a good salary. Self-educated and conversant on numerous topics, he had previously worked in the Brazilian senate and Ministry of Justice, so he understood the law as well. I admired his vast knowledge, despite his limited schooling, and the ease and self-confidence with which he worked.

Wanting to support a family in the manner to which Rudá had become accustomed, I wrote to my old junior high school, Belisário dos Santos, and returned quickly to my studies. Rudá stood by me for the next several years as I worked full time during the day and studied at night. We dated for several more years and decided to get married in 1956. It was a difficult year for me. I had finished junior high school and was in my first phase of high school studies (*segundo grau*), sleeping little and trying to earn enough money for our wedding, which we decided would take place on December 7. My comfort lay in Rudá, who became more dear to me each day, delightful, tender, confident in our future, and determined to overcome the obstacles in our path.

We had found and rented a small apartment in an area near the center of Rio called Flamengo in preparation for our marriage. Our new home consisted of one very small room with a tiny alcove at the back in which we put a two-burner stove. That was the kitchen. We earned enough money for a small collapsible table to eat on, accompanied by two unpainted stools from the street market, and a few other meager furnishings, including a hide-a-bed sofa. It was all we had—and a marked contrast to the comforts of Rudá's affluent home.

Finally, our wedding day arrived, an unexpectedly traumatic day for me. The first part of the wedding took place on December 7, a civil marriage required by Brazilian law to occur before the religious ceremony. That day it rained and rained. The courthouse was packed with couples like us who wanted to be married on December 8, the

Catholic holiday *O Dia da Nossa Senhora da Conceição*. We finally were married and returned to Rudá's home in the late afternoon, where I left my new bride and rushed back to school. In order to advance, all students needed to pass a special exam in each subject, and I was now late for my oral test in biology.

As I arrived, the exam board was getting ready to conclude. "You are late. Where is your sense of responsibility?" the board's president asked sternly. When I explained about my marriage and the large number of couples at the courthouse, another member of the board, much to my surprise, mentioned that he had also gotten married that day. Because he felt sympathetic to my situation, the board bent the rules. Their feeling of empathy and goodwill put me at ease. I went on to get the best grade I ever received in biology.

The next day, December 8, 1956, Rudá and I were married in the Santo Antônio dos Pobres church on Invalidos Street in the center of Rio. My father dressed in his best suit, but was a mere shadow of his former self, the effects of illness continuing to daunt him. He had high blood pressure and appeared thin and bent over. My mother, nervous and timid, wore a new dress and new shoes. The only other member of my family to attend the wedding was my brother Honório. Together we took two buses to arrive at Rudá's home. As we walked up the stairs, the heel on my mother's shoe broke and she became even more nervous and embarrassed.

Helvécio and Rudá on their wedding day, December 8, 1956

©The Church of Jesus Christ of Latter-day Saints. First published in the *Friend*, January 1992. Used by permission.

Rudá's family received us warmly and we left for Santo Antônio dos Pobres, an exquisite church with gold-plated figures gracing the ceiling. The ceremony included all the grandeur of a typical Brazilian Catholic wedding, but the high point for me was the moment Rudá entered the church. I was so moved at seeing her in her beautiful wedding dress that I started to weep, unable to contain my tears even as we greeted guests after the wedding. I had finally realized a long-awaited, wonderful dream.

Later that day, however, an even more powerful emotion overwhelmed me when Rudá's mother greeted us back at her home. Rudá and I entered the dining room and my new mother-in-law immediately gave me an unforgettably strong and loving embrace. That hug conveyed, without words, her acceptance, love, approval, and blessing. At that moment, I no longer had a mother-in-law, but another mother. Future events would confirm that impression, for she became a wonderful, supportive friend to me. When my own mother died eight years after the wedding, Rudá's mother took over that role and accepted me as her own son. Her attention to me, in fact, created some jealousy among other family members, but she maintained our wonderful relationship until the day she passed away.

Her good nature and hospitality were extended to us immediately. Rudá and I spent our honeymoon, for lack of money, in our tiny apartment, with only a few days off work. When Rudá became homesick, I suggested that we call her family. We didn't own a phone, so I dialed her mother on a nearby pay phone. "Dona (Mrs.) Margarita, this is Helvécio. How are you doing?" I asked when she answered. Rudá's mother responded cheerfully, "Good, how are you and Rudá?"

"Rudá misses you. Would it be all right if we came by to visit?"

"Yes, please come as soon as you can and stay for dinner."

She received us both with warm embraces in her typical loving way and we enjoyed a wonderful evening. I received so much affection from that woman that I get upset when someone speaks poorly of mother-in-laws. I didn't have a mother-in-law. I had a second mother.

THE SHALLOWNESS OF SUCCESS

The fifteen years or so after my marriage could be characterized, in worldly terms, as my rise to success. Through study, hard work, and a determination to support my family, I went from the obscure position of an errand-boy to that of a prosperous corporate executive. Rudá and I began with our cramped quarters and ended up in a spacious apartment, enjoying frequent invitations to social gatherings for the country's elite. Brazil's president and I became friends on a first-name basis and I possessed national prominence and influence. I must also credit a factor beyond my control for my professional climb: Brazil's racial tolerance. Especially during the 1950s and 60s, my race proved much less of a barrier in Brazil than it would have been elsewhere, and never posed a problem to me.

Back in the early days of our marriage, Rudá and I could not have imagined the gradual transformation yet to occur in our lives. Adaptation to married life was somewhat difficult for Rudá, accustomed as she was to the

THE SHALLOWNESS OF SUCCESS

comforts of her parents' beautiful home—comforts such as her own room and a good bed. Even so, we happily worked and adjusted to our lives together. After waking early, we would ride the streetcar together to Carioca Plaza where the female street vendors from the northern Brazilian state of Bahia sold *carajé* and *cocadas*. Wearing their traditional white dresses, the women sold their delicacies on large trays called *tabuleiros*. The architect of the trolley station actually used the *tabuleiro* as his model for the building; from a distance, the station did, in fact, look like a tray.

After working all day, we would meet in the city for some brief time together before Rudá returned home on the trolley and I went off to school. Finally, at around ten at night, I would return home for a simple, delicious meal Rudá had prepared for us. She was constantly concerned about me. We enjoyed talking to each other and listening to the radio together after a long day.

We also thoroughly enjoyed our remarkable city. Rio de Janeiro had much less crime and fewer social problems back then. True, slums (*favelas*), poverty, and their attendant woes have always resided within Rio's resplendent landscape. But the city seemed calmer then—the criminals consisting of small-time pickpockets instead of street bandits with guns. On Saturdays, Rudá and I would go to the movies at midnight, walking home at two in the morning without being threatened or accosted in any way. Going down the silent, deserted streets talking,

27

all we could hear were the sound of our voices and our own footsteps.

Rio's buildings, parks, and infrastructure changed over the years as well. Rudá and I enjoyed a small park in Flamengo, which later became a much larger Flamengo Park after Governor Carlos Lacerda ordered the leveling of Santo Antônio Hill. The dirt and rock from the hill then was used to build up the Flamengo Beach area, and now the larger park houses the Museum of Modern Art and a monument to the Brazilian military expedition in Italy.

Tunnels through the mountains, underpasses, and viaducts further modernized the city. And in 1956, when Juscelino Kubitschek was elected president, construction began for a new capital city to replace Rio de Janeiro: Brasília, a city much further inland which would hopefully draw Brazil's populace in from the crowded coastline. Thus Rio lost its status as the Federal District in 1960 and became a state, with Carlos Lacerda, a combative journalist, the newly elected governor. We enjoyed watching our city progress and always thought of it as an exciting, good place to live.

In 1958, Rudá and I decided to begin a family and, later that year, Rudá announced she was expecting a child. We were thrilled. But our happiness soon gave way to concern as Rudá became ill. She finally had to quit her job and spent most of her time under her mother's care at her parents' house, since I was away at work. One day her father asked, "Why are you renting an apartment when you are here most of the time?" He felt that we might as well move in with them and save our rent money to buy an apartment of our own. We gladly took him up on his offer and saved our money in the months to come.

The year 1959 ended up being a much better year for Rudá and me than the preceding one: our family welcomed a son and I entered college, although the former was a more traumatic accomplishment for Rudá than the latter was for me. Rudá had been sick, of course, but we still planned on a normal birth. Things don't always go as planned. On April 22, 1959, Rudá went into early labor brought on by the shock of seeing her nephew fall down the stairs. At the hospital, the doctor informed us that the baby was not positioned correctly for a normal birth, and he tried different procedures all day long to turn the baby around.

Finally, after receiving our permission, the doctor wheeled Rudá into the operating room for a cesarean section as my mother-in-law and I worriedly waited. When we heard the first cry of a baby, we couldn't contain our emotions and began crying ourselves. The doctor came out and told us that Rudá had come through the operation well and that we had a healthy baby boy. Marcus Helvécio was a joy to us from the beginning. In that same eventful year, I finished high school and took written and oral entrance examinations for the College of Finance and Economics of Rio de Janeiro. I passed them all—Portuguese, math, geography, economics, and

Brazilian political history—and was accepted. Life seemed complete.

But it never quite is. Several months after Marcus's birth, my father became seriously ill. We went to visit him in Irajá, where he wanted to hold Marcus in his arms, but was too weak even for that. Later on in the year, my boss told me to go home from work. "Your father is very ill," he said. I arrived home too late. That morning, my father had returned home from a walk with my nephew, Mauro, and lay down to rest. He asked my mother for a glass of water and by the time she returned from the kitchen, he had quietly died.

My father was my idol. Whenever I drive with my children on President Vargas Avenue in Rio with its four wide lanes of traffic, I always remind them that we are driving over the sweat of their grandfather. He was a man who received very little recognition for his hard work and dignity, and his success could hardly be measured in terms of wealth or fortune. But he was a man of great dignity and self-respect. I know of nothing that could be said against his good name.

I only wish my relationship with my father could have been closer. We were always somewhat distant because of the work and time constraints he operated under his whole life. We talked, but never had time to develop the relationship I wanted. For this reason, I yearn for the day when I will meet my father on the other side of the veil, where I can embrace him and tell

THE SHALLOWNESS OF SUCCESS

him how much I love, respect, and honor him. I always wanted to give my children the type of paternal relationship that life's difficulties robbed from me.

Our financial condition improved as I continued to work hard, always trying to put my family's well-being on a more secure foundation. In 1959, we moved to Meier, Rudá's family's neighborhood, and into a new apartment complete with a refrigerator and a television. Then in 1962, I graduated from college and, at the encouragement of several university friends, applied to work at Petrobras, the government-owned oil firm established by Getúlio Vargas. One of Brazil's largest companies, Petrobras controlled almost all of the oil and gas activities in the country, so I felt fortunate, at age thirty-two, to be offered a job there in a newly established financial division. One year later, I became head of the new department, receiving not only an elevated status in the company, but also a much better salary.

The higher position also necessitated dealing with members of Brazil's highly volatile labor unions. Especially during my early years with Petrobras, the unions were particularly militant and disruptive, for yet another political crisis had erupted in Brazil. Jánio Quadros had resigned as president of Brazil in 1961, after which congress stripped his vice-president, João Goulart, of a great deal of power before allowing him to assume the presidency. Labor unions, whom Goulart had ingratiated while working under President Vargas, constantly worked for a nation-wide strike in support of Goulart, and staged strikes in every sector of society. We had no idea what would happen from one day to the next. Food and utility shortages, popular unrest, and constant agitation reigned during this three-year period.

The oil industry labor unions wielded a great deal of power. Their leaders figured prominently in the national labor movement and aspired to establish a "labor republic" in Brazil, one in which the labor unions controlled the government. Since Petrobras constituted one of the largest firms in the country, union leaders focused their attention on the company, turning it into one of the centers of labor unrest in Brazil. The year 1963 was a particularly difficult year: production dropped sharply and stoppages occurred throughout the company. The outlook for the country was bleak.

The union leaders employed methods that exacerbated the company's unrest and dwindling activity. They possessed more power than Petrobras's management team and could stop work to hold labor meetings whenever they wanted. The issues discussed in the meetings focused on political agendas that often had little to do with company productivity. I found labor politics, especially the way in which the leaders attracted supporters, very disagreeable and tried to stay out of their disputes. I didn't fight them, in part to protect myself, but I didn't support them either.

Unfortunately, the labor unions eventually caught up with me. Since I presided over a relatively important

THE SHALLOWNESS OF SUCCESS

department, they wanted me on their side and assigned a labor leader to persuade me to support their cause. He visited me at least twice a day, making me stop work to review their political platform and ideas of the future labor government. Day after day, over and over again, he came and expounded on the same ideas, stressing the advantages for those who became affiliated with their case early on in the process. He also indicated that I could become one of the leaders, but I was not impressed with their ideas and offered no response. For me, their ideology was little more than rhetoric.

The labor union's attempts to recruit me ended when the leaders unjustly accused an employee I supervised, claiming he affiliated with an opposing right-wing party, the Integralists, and that he worked against the labor movement. It wasn't true. He was just a family man, like me, who didn't want to get involved. But since the employee had no position or authority, they wouldn't tolerate him like they tolerated me. They wanted him fired.

I vigorously defended the man and the union consequently turned against me—viciously. The union leader assigned to recruit me even attacked me with racial slurs. "Look Helvécio," he warned, "your days are numbered. Remember, you are a black. When the labor government takes over, you can be sure they will deport you to Alabama, where all blacks belong!" That all blacks should be sent to Alabama was a common racist saying at the time.

Map of Brazil showing locations mentioned in the book.

THE SHALLOWNESS OF SUCCESS

The union leader, however, never visited me again after that. Tranquillity returned to the country and to my company in 1964 when a military government deposed João Goulart. The new system restored peace and tranquillity, and stayed in power for the next twenty-five years. Meanwhile, Petrobras, now liberated from the constant demands and threats of the unions, returned to the business of oil production. As the company expanded, important administrative changes occurred, all of which increased production and allowed qualified people to move up in the company.

I greatly benefited from these changes, and my ascent up the corporate ladder began. First, I became head of accounting, then later head of finances, for my division. Then, Petrobras paid for me to take post-graduate finance and administration courses at the Getúlio Vargas Institute, as well as classes at the Catholic Pontificate University (*Pontifice Universidade Católica*) in Rio de Janeiro. This postgraduate work not only qualified me for jobs in general administration, but also enabled me to obtain a broad understanding of the responsibilities of a company executive.

By 1968, Rudá and I had saved enough money to buy our first apartment. Located on Intendente Cunha Meneses Street, it had large, spacious rooms, and we were very happy there. At the same time, I also embarked upon a teaching career. I received a teacher education diploma from the Getúlio Vargas Institute, and while still working as a Petrobras administrator, I accepted a position to teach part time at the State University of Rio de Janeiro School of Finances and Administration. There, I shared my knowledge of the professional world with the students while developing my own skills in a university setting. Coordinating teaching with my job proved difficult, initially, but the routine became easier with time.

Things were coming together in many ways—a little girl, Marisa Helena, had joined our family, we had a new home, new opportunities. Then a serious automobile accident nearly derailed my life. Returning to work one day in July 1969, I distinctly remember the voice of my chauffeur stating, "Sir, that car ran a red light and is going to hit us." I looked up from my newspaper and then blanked out as a car violently collided into mine, throwing my driver out of the car. He suffered broken arms, a broken jaw, and abrasions, while I remained trapped in the car as it rolled several times. I suffered a concussion and a broken back, and lay unconscious and paralyzed in the hospital for a week.

The doctors predicted that, in the unlikely event that I survived, I would have serious physical handicaps. For sixty days a plaster cast covered me from my waist to my head, allowing my face to peek out. For another three months I wore a neck cast. Finally, after so many months in a cast, I wanted to go back to work. The doctors refused, declaring me so badly injured that I would have to remain inactive for another year.

THE SHALLOWNESS OF SUCCESS

Not be able to work constituted a terrible punishment for me. Even tranquilizers and sleeping pills could not help me to sleep. But finally, in January, I received permission to work on a limited basis, working two hours a day during the first week and an additional hour each succeeding week. I followed this schedule for one day. The next day I worked all day, and, to my great relief, slept all night. I decided that working a regular schedule was worth the risk.

After my quite miraculous recovery, another major career move occurred in February of 1970. Petrobras promoted me to their commercial department, an important division involving importation-exportation, price setting, and all other financial aspects of oil, as well as the political issues of its supply and distribution. The general superintendent said he had heard good things about me and wanted me in his department. I, in turn, was elated at the prospects of a new job, for I knew my current job responsibilities inside and out and yearned for fresh challenges.

This promotion led to an even bigger opportunity when a commercial sub-department, involved in the retailing of oil derivatives, began growing in importance. The sub-division had succeeded in making Petrobras competitive in the domestic commercial market amongst such international giants as Esso, Shell, Texaco, and Plantia, among others. So, logically, Petrobras formed a committee to organize the sub-division into a subsidiary company responsible for all the distribution of oil derivative products. Because I formed part of the organizing committee, many were surprised that, when the new company began functioning in 1972, I was not transferred to work there. But I didn't let the decision bother me and continued with my duties.

Three months after the subsidiary's initial organization, a Petrobras vice-president and the new company's financial director asked me to head the subsidiary's division of financial planning. One month later, I became the head of financing. In this position, I frequently worked with the national government agency on oil, headquartered in Brasília, and often attended meetings on issues of great importance.

The year was 1972. I had an excellent salary, led a department of over two-hundred employees, worked directly under Petrobras's board of directors, socialized with the country's elite, and had achieved great professional success. Yet Rudá and I were unhappy. Much of the time, I felt emotionally drained and irritable. I would go to work feeling confused and return home feeling agitated. Why? No logical explanation existed. Rudá was everything I could ask for in a wife—loving, beautiful, a marvelous mother. We had our two wonderful children: Marcus had turned thirteen and Marisa Helena was six. My job afforded a home, neighborhood, and lifestyle far above anything I had ever dreamed of while growing up. But despite all the success, neither of us was satisfied with our lives.

CONVERSION

The emotional emptiness that ironically accompanied my ascent in the corporate world, I now know with certainty, stemmed from spiritual confusion. Even back then, Rudá and I knew deep inside that somehow, something was wrong with our spiritual lives. In the early 1970s, we had become, at the encouragement of Rudá's family, active participants in a spiritualist religion known as Macumba. Yet we had always felt uneasy about the religion's ideology and practices. Macumba makes up part of a strong Brazilian religious tradition based on the early beliefs of the African slaves, combined with elements of the Catholic church, French spiritualism, and local Brazilian folk traditions. In Rio, Macumba is especially popular. Among its many tenets is the belief in communication with spirits of the dead, communication that usually occurs in religious ceremonies replete with music and dancing.

Rudá and I attended Macumba meetings almost every Saturday. In fact, I even served as treasurer for our group. Other members encouraged me to run for vice-president in an upcoming election, but we felt too uneasy about our association to become that involved. Leaving Macumba, however, proves difficult for those who want out: bad things always happen, the members warn, to those who leave. Even our fear of repercussions, though, didn't prevent us from gradually missing meetings.

We finally decided to leave the group altogether when, after Rudá's mother died, the group held a séance. Over the course of the meeting, Rudá's older sister was supposedly possessed by the spirit of my mother-in-law. When vulgarity spewed from her mouth, Rudá and I realized that this "spirit" could not be the woman we knew as Rudá's mother. The whole thing was a sham. We decided that very day never to return.

But our spiritual confusion continued. Rudá and I talked often about our predicament and concluded that we needed to develop a relationship with God and our Savior, Jesus Christ. So we began frequenting various Christian denominations. We knew the most about Catholicism and began attending Mass. Colleagues at the university also invited us to attend various Protestant services, which we did: Methodist, Baptist, Presbyterian, and Anglican. Still, nothing was different. Still, something was missing.

Our lives only began to change when I made my first feeble attempt to contact the source of all truth—God—in what couldn't exactly be called a prayer. It was more of a cry for help. One night I got stuck in a traffic jam on the way home from work. The cars—all stopped in an area called Maracanã, near the world's largest soccer stadium—seemed motionless in an interminably long line. So, with the moon and stars shining on a clear April night, I got out of the car and looked up at the sky.

"My God," I thought, "I know you are there some place, but I don't know where. Is it possible you don't see the confusion my family and I are experiencing? Is it possible you don't realize we are searching for something and that we don't even know what it is? Why don't you help us? Why don't you help us find that something which will bring relief, satisfaction, joy?"

After I had uttered my plea, the traffic cleared up and I returned home, quickly forgetting about the incident. But Heavenly Father had not forgotten. I had prayed as earnestly as I knew how to at the time, and my request had been heard. Two weeks later we returned from a short trip to Belo Horizonte to find a nicely printed card under our door. On one side was a painting of Christ; on the other, a meeting schedule for a local chapel. Missionaries from The Church of Jesus Christ of Latter-day Saints had left the card.

Intrigued, I took the card to work the next day and told my assistants, "Look at this card I found under my door, about the church on Maxwell Street. I would like to go there."

One of them replied, "That is a church for North Americans. If you don't know a member, I wouldn't even try to go, because you can only enter with another member. They won't let you in." Because I had been a member of the Free Masons for several years and knew that the only way to enter a Masonic meeting was to attend with a member, I assumed the Church operated the same way. Consequently I didn't even try to go to the LDS church.

However, the Lord had heard my request on that unusual night and wanted to help me. A few days later, two missionaries came to our apartment. I was in a terrible mood that night after a frustrating day at work and, after a brief hello, told Rudá: "I don't want to see anybody. I don't even want dinner. I'm going to take a shower and go to bed. If someone calls, I'm not home." So Rudá quickly informed the children that Daddy was not to be bothered and they went to their rooms.

The doorbell rang after I had changed my clothes. I hurriedly headed for the bathroom, telling Rudá, "Remember, I'm not home!" But something persuaded me to leave the door open just a crack and I clearly heard Rudá's voice saying, "Yes, he would like to talk to you, but he is tired and taking a shower. Then he's going right to bed. Could you possibly come back some other day?" I didn't hear the response, but after the visitor left I asked Rudá who had come. She replied that those "two young men from that church you wanted to visit" had just come, and I cried, "Go and bring them back!" She scurried down into the street and retrieved the young men. It was around eight-thirty in the evening.

CONVERSION

Into my home came Elder Thomas McIntire from California, the older of the two missionaries, and his companion, Elder Steve Richards, from Atlanta, Georgia. Elder McIntire was obviously nervous when he saw me, a big, tall black man standing in the middle of the living room with his hands on his hips. But I, on the other hand, was feeling much better. In fact, the moment those two young men stepped into our apartment, all of my gloom and spiritual discomfort immediately disappeared and was replaced by a calm and serenity which I now know came from the influence of the Holy Spirit. An extraordinary feeling of relief overcame me as I greeted those missionaries and invited my two children into the room.

After everyone was seated, the missionaries said they were representatives of the Lord Jesus Christ and that they had a blessing for our family if we would like one. I told them yes, but stated that I first had some questions I would like them to answer. First we talked in general terms about the Church. Then I asked a question I now realize God had prepared these young men spiritually to handle. I also realize now that God had prepared me and my family to hear their response. "Given that your church is headquartered in the United States," I began, "a country with a history of racial conflict, how does your religion treat blacks? Are they allowed into the church?" The year was 1972—six years prior to the priesthood revelation allowing blacks to hold the priesthood.

Elder McIntire initially went red in the face and nervously squirmed in his chair. Then, he asked our permission to have a prayer, which we agreed to, and afterward began giving what I now realize was the first missionary discussion. The elders continued talking. I kept asking questions, the most pertinent of which they responded to. Before we knew it, the hour was one in the morning, and those missionaries had given us, I again realize in retrospect, most of the missionary lessons. During that four-and-a-half-hour discussion, we dealt with the issue of blacks and the priesthood. The missionaries' explanation seemed clear to me and, more important, I accepted the practice as the will of the Lord.

Before leaving, Elder McIntire asked if I would pray. We knelt together, the missionaries and my family, and I gave my first unmemorized public prayer. A testimony began to grow in all of our hearts that night, and we made another appointment with the elders. Late as it was, my wife and I continued to talk about all we had heard. We had found answers to our questions. We weren't confused and upset anymore. Calmness, serenity, and happiness had entered our home.

During the second discussion a few days later, the missionaries invited us to attend church. This was back in the days when Sunday School took place in the morning, sacrament meeting at night. So, on the following Sunday, after getting up late, as usual, we decided to attend the six o'clock sacrament meeting. When we

CONVERSION

arrived at the chapel on Joaquim Meia Street, everyone was already inside the building, which looked more like a dilapidated old house. I learned later that legal problems had prevented the Church from carrying out its construction of a new chapel. For the time being, Rio Saints in the area met under a ceiling that looked as though it could cave in at any moment.

The meeting, however, far surpassed its humble setting. Rudá and I had never been to a more interesting service. After Elders McIntire and Richards enthusiastically greeted us, we found a seat while every eye in the congregation fixed on us—had everyone waited for our arrival before commencing the meeting? It seemed that way. The messages in the talks focused on motherhood, since it was Mother's Day, and afterwards the women, including Rudá, received a rose. As we got up to leave, most of the congregation greeted us warmly, and Branch President Antônio Landelino de Barros, who lived on our street, offered to help us with anything we needed. What a beautiful experience. The spirit of the talks, the feeling of the meeting, the love of the members—everything confirmed that we had found the true church.

Little by little, we began to change as we gradually overcame old habits and faithfully attended church meetings and activities. The branch president brought over home teachers and explained the home teaching program. His dedication taught me a great deal, and I remembered his example when I became a Church leader.

45

The missionaries, ward members, and especially our own fasting and prayers all helped us immensely in gaining a testimony of the restored gospel. But still, we remained nervous about getting baptized, mostly due to a fear, later validated, of our extended families' negative reactions.

Two events, however, changed our hearts and gave us the spiritual courage we lacked. The first took place at a large meeting of the Rio de Janeiro District in the Tijuca chapel. From the first chords of the prelude music to the closing prayer, a powerful spirit filled the meeting. Brother Val Carter, a counselor in the Brazil North Mission presidency, bore his testimony about the mission of the Savior, declaring his complete dependence upon Jesus Christ for his salvation and exaltation. His words profoundly touched my heart and my entire being. I couldn't control my emotions and was surprised to find myself in tears. The Holy Ghost confirmed to us that The Church of Jesus Christ of Latter-day Saints was the kingdom of God on earth.

At that moment, a miracle occurred: our fear of baptism disappeared. We only needed to commit ourselves to a date, which, after a second powerful experience, came easily. As we drove home pensively from Sunday School the next week, Marcus, thirteen at the time, broke the silence. "We are different now," he said. "Your faces glow, and I know what is causing it: the gospel of Jesus Christ. I don't know what you are going to do, but I have already decided to get baptized."

CONVERSION

I stopped the car and we broke down and cried. When we returned for sacrament meeting, we ran into the branch president's office. He began talking about baptism as I began explaining that we wanted to get baptized. The following week, on June 2, 1972, Rudá, Marcus, and I entered the fold of Christ through the door of baptism. Marisa Helena joined us later when she turned eight. Through obeying the laws of the gospel, fasting, and serving, we had received the ability to overcome the fear and challenges that kept us from joining the Church. We also knew that through following the same principles, Heavenly Father would help us overcome any obstacles to progressing in the kingdom.

One obstacle that definitely didn't exist for us was a lack of support from fellow members. In the weeks that followed our baptism and beyond, branch members showed a tremendous amount of concern, caring, and love for us—just as they did to everyone who came. In fact, I have seen few places in the Church where fellowshipping was as effective and sincere as in that branch. Everyone called each other brother and sister and truly felt a familial tie in that atmosphere of acceptance and support.

Initially, I wondered if our family received special treatment because I was a Petrobras executive and university professor. But as we became more and more involved, I clearly saw that such was not the case. When the traditional Brazilian holiday *São João* came around,

47

Rudá and I worked on the organizing committee for the activity. Assigned to the soft-drink booth, I had to dig holes with a pick for the booth's wooden frame. My hands, soft and unaccustomed to labor after years at a desk, blistered and bled. But I appreciated the chance to work hard. After we sold all the drinks, I worked at the games booth, and that successful party was a memorable occasion for me. We all did our part together.

Our local Church leaders took an extremely important step in helping us progress by allowing us to serve. In fact, I had a rather auspicious induction into the world of church callings after my baptism. Just as I was trying to reconcile myself to the fact that, for two years, I would have to attend the class for new members and visitors in Sunday School, the branch president called me in for an appointment. "Brother Martins, I have a calling for you," he began, after shutting the door to his office. "The Lord wants you to be the gospel doctrine teacher in Sunday School for the long-time members."

I felt as though I had been struck by lightning. "How could I ever teach that class," I pled, "having only been a member of the Church for one week?"

"It's the will of the Lord," he replied. "You'll have to decide whether to accept it." After hearing that, I humbly accepted the calling. "Who am I," I reasoned, "to go against the will of the Lord?" I put my trust in him and experienced a very emotional moment when my name was announced in sacrament meeting as the new gospel doctrine teacher.

The course of study centered on the Articles of Faith, but the branch had no manual. So, after hearing about the Church Distribution Center in São Paulo, I flew south to that huge city that week, taking a taxi directly from the airport to the Church offices in the Vila Olímpia district. There, I met two people who became my close friends: Sister Maria José, the wife of former São Paulo West Stake President Harry Eduardo Klein, and José Benjamin Puerta, who later became president of the São Paulo Temple. They greeted me and helped me as I purchased every Church publication available, including the teacher's manual. I flew back to Rio with a large package in tow.

Through teaching, and studying all of my material, I learned a great deal. Rudá was immediately called to serve also, as a counselor in the Primary presidency. Together we gained a testimony of church callings and their importance to church activity. A few weeks after being called as the gospel doctrine teacher, I woke up one Sunday so sick with the flu I could barely get out of bed. "I can't make it to church today," I thought. But then a nonmember friend whom I had invited to attend my class appeared at the door. When I saw him, I thought of others in my class, especially those to whom I had given assignments to participate, and how I would be disappointing them if I didn't show up. I suddenly realized I had made a commitment to the Lord and to the branch members, and that realization gave me the strength to get up and go to church. I then gave what was probably one of the best Sunday School lessons I have ever given.

Without my calling, I would have stayed home. Then, on another day for a less important reason, I might have stayed home again, beginning a pattern of inactivity that many can, and do, fall into. Elder James E. Faust once observed that in the ruins of Athens, only the columns with weight upon them had survived the ravages of time. He compared the columns to Church members, for we need to have the weight of responsibility on us to stay active, learning, praying, and developing through our callings. I testify to the importance of giving recently baptized members positions that are at least equal to their level of ability and supporting them in their efforts to serve.

Soon after I was baptized, another opportunity to participate helped solidify my commitment to the Church. Valdemar Cury, the Rio district president, and George Oaks, the mission president, invited me to speak at the Rio de Janeiro district conference. Can you imagine? I had been a Church member for one month and had limited understanding of Church doctrine. I'm sure they were apprehensive about what kinds of things I would say to so many members. But I'm very grateful these good leaders took a risk and let me have the experience of

CONVERSION

bearing my testimony not just to my Sunday School class or to my branch, but to all of the attending members in Rio de Janeiro. The experience was unforgettable, and my love for the gospel and my fellow members grew immensely.

Because of the members' help and the leadership's willingness to give us callings, our adaptation to Church life was untraumatic. Not so, however, for our adjustment to joining a religion different from that of Rudá's family. My family, fortunately, had accepted our announcement of baptism without serious objection. My parents had passed away and I, being the oldest, had a strong influence over my younger brothers and sisters. I had also attained the highest level of education, so they never felt as though they could go against me to openly oppose the decision of a sibling they respected. But Rudá's family was different. Our announcement to them of joining the LDS Church had the effect of dropping a bomb. They exerted strong pressure on Rudá and the children, who were in constant contact with them, to abandon our new faith.

In order to preserve the tranquillity of the family, we tried to distance ourselves by moving from Rudá's family's neighborhood to the Tijuca district. A day before our sixteenth wedding anniversary, December 6, 1972, Rudá and I moved with our children to 500 Conde de Bomfim Street. There, we escaped the intense pressure of Rudá's relatives, but made sure that we didn't abandon the family altogether. Yet, family members still did what they could to keep us away from church activity. Birthday parties and celebrations suddenly began occurring on Sundays. After recognizing their strategy, we visited family members on Saturdays, or on their real birthdays, to pay our respects.

We also tried to be the first to help if any family member fell ill, and over time our concern and love for them have led most of the family to hold the Church in high regard. No one has yet been baptized, but they now actually try to help us, rather than hinder us, in following our religion. No longer do family members put alcoholic drinks out on special occasions, and at dinners, no one begins eating until my father-in-law asks me to offer a prayer.

The culmination of the growing goodwill between both of our families occurred in 1978, after black Latter-day Saint males had been given the priesthood. My sister-in-law's grandson had arrived three months premature, without much chance of surviving. The baby's mother, having heard about priesthood blessings for the sick, asked Rudá if I would bless her son. I agreed and blessed him in the intensive care unit of the hospital. Today the boy is healthy and strong. When he reached three or four years old, his mother even requested that he be blessed in the Church.

Our conversion, then, didn't necessitate breaking ties with our family. We just had to change our interaction in some respects. But we did, after baptism, decide to openly and officially break ties with former doctrines. I wrote a letter to the *Centro Espírita* declaring our new beliefs, and officially severed our connection with Macumba. I also ended my participation in Free Masonry.

Because I had ascended to the higher levels of the organization, the Masonic fraternity greatly encouraged my return to activity, visiting me at home and work and inviting me to dinner. But I never swerved in my position. The gospel of Jesus Christ had filled my heart and mind so completely, I felt my spirit had no room for other types of philosophies. The Masons persisted, however, only halting their reactivation efforts when I began inviting them to church. For every invitation I received to attend a Masonic meeting, I responded with an invitation to attend our ward. This method soon discouraged them, but I remain friends to this day with several Masons. Whenever I was called to a leadership position in the Church, I invited my Masonic friends to lunch and, after explaining what was happening in my life, encouraged them to investigate the Church. Unfortunately, none of them have yet accepted this challenge.

As we continued to live the commandments to the best of our ability, meaningful spiritual experiences strengthened our faith and testimonies. One such experience happened when our district became the first stake in Rio de Janeiro. Elder Bruce R. McConkie came to Brazil as a new apostle for his first conference as a member of the Council of the Twelve and spoke to an enormous congregation in the Adarai chapel. People sat in chair-filled hallways and in the cultural hall—anywhere, in fact, where they could find room. Elder McConkie's talk was unforgettable.

A seminary choir, including Marcus Helvécio, provided the music, and afterwards, we had the wonderful experience of having our picture taken with Elder McConkie. President Cury of the district became our new stake president, with Antônio Almeida Costa and Oscar Batista de Carvalho his counselors, and Walmir Silva the stake patriarch. I was called as a counselor in the stake Sunday School presidency and Rudá as a counselor in the stake Primary presidency.

The new stake was vast. Its far-flung boundaries posed an enormous geographical challenge to us as stake leaders trying to visit various wards and train leaders. From the Paraiba Valley in the state of Rio, up the mountain to the cities of Petrópolis, Teresópolis, and Nova Friburgo, and clear into the state of Minas Gerais, we visited different wards and branches every Sunday. Because Primary in those days occurred on a week day, the stake Primary presidency traveled midweek. Often, we husbands would be waiting at the bus terminal after eleven o'clock at night or later, expecting our wives to return from their visits. Yet nobody complained of the distances we traveled—not even the Primary presidency who often stayed out very late. We were happy to do the work.

With Rudá and children, in front of the Rio de Janeiro stake center, 1978.

As we adjusted to life as a Mormon family, we found ourselves throwing out the bad in our former lifestyle while trying to only retain the positive and uplifting. In the first few months after our baptism, we would watch television between and after church meetings on Sunday. Then, after listening to a lesson in church on keeping the Sabbath day holy, we decided that, for us, the day would be more sacred without television. A challenge arose that very night when, as we rode up the elevator to our apartment after church, we recalled that a John Wayne western would be on TV that night. I am a big John Wayne fan. "Dad," Marcus asked hopefully, "do we have to begin today?" I answered, "Yes. If we start today, then from today on, we will never watch television on Sunday."

We also learned in another lesson that adhering to the Word of Wisdom means not only that we should live by its precepts, but also that we should help others live by them as well. Because of my position at Petrobras, we customarily received expensive liquors as Christmas presents. "We'll just give these bottles to friends and family members who drink," I had reasoned after I was baptized. But after the lesson, Marcus, Rudá, and I had a discussion—after which we turned on the faucet, opened all the bottles, and poured the alcohol down the drain, famous imported brands and all. Interestingly, from that day forward, we never again received liquor as a present.

As we continued coming to and participating in the Church, many members seemed amazed, even sometimes shocked, that we, as blacks, could stay active without holding the priesthood. Some expressed surprise that we didn't lapse into inactivity, and rarely a week went by without someone asking us how we felt about not holding the priesthood. Finally, I researched and studied the question, not for personal interest or because I harbored doubts, but simply in order to respond adequately to the many who were curious about the Church's position. Frequently Church leaders asked us to bear our testimonies at firesides and even speak to groups about the doctrine of the priesthood.

As for Rudá, myself, and my family, we knew the Church was true, and that was all that mattered. Yet others seemed agitated by our family's lack of concern over the priesthood policy. "If I were in your situation," said one member, "I don't believe I would stay in the Church." I replied that I was sorry to hear that, but was sure that, were he in my situation, he would feel differently. Our bishop once remarked, "Helvécio, I believe your greatest challenge is to stay in the Church without the priesthood."

I responded by saying, "Bishop, I would be grateful if it were my greatest trial. Of course, I realize that I could serve in many more ways with the priesthood, but I in no way feel inferior without it. In fact, I feel things are a bit easier for me compared to you and all of your responsibilities. The Lord expects a great deal from you as a priesthood holder. I sincerely pray for you and want you to always remember your duty. My family and I are dependent upon your priesthood. Remain worthy and faithful and we will always enjoy the blessings you have for us."

There were even some members, fortunately only a few, who seemed bothered by our devoutness. Oddly enough, they criticized our struggle to live the things we were taught, and even mockingly asked questions about our beliefs. While we felt concern for these members, we did not allow their uncharitable attitudes to affect our activity in the Church. We continued to do what we felt was the Lord's will and to appreciate the good example of the many faithful members we knew.

We also greatly appreciated the example and inspiration of the General Authorities whom we had the privilege to hear and see back in the early days of the Church in Rio. In 1973, Rudá and I experienced the first in a series of unforgettable meetings with Elder Spencer W. Kimball, then President of the Quorum of the Twelve Apostles. We listened to him at a Saturday night meeting of a special conference and couldn't take our eyes off him as he came down the aisle at the meeting's conclusion. When President Kimball came to where we were seated at the end of a row, he stopped. My wife and I stood up as he shook our hands, greeted us, and pointed at Marcus Helvécio in the choir, asking if he were our son. After I said yes, that wonderful man—with whom we were to share several remarkable incidents in the years to come—smiled. He wished us well and walked away.

CONVERSION

Then, in 1974, another opportunity arose to meet a very special leader. I was sitting at home during a stake priesthood leadership meeting when the telephone rang. The stake president wanted to know if Rudá and I would come to the chapel because Elder James E. Faust, then an assistant to the Twelve, wanted to talk to us. My wife became extremely nervous. "What does he want with us?" she wondered. Later, when Elder Faust invited us into an office, he could see that she was nervous. I told him Rudá had said earlier, "If I had an interview with a General Authority, I would probably faint from fear." But we went on to have an enjoyable interview with Elder Faust, after which he said, "Now Rudá, you are still alive, and you didn't die or even faint!"

We left without knowing the reason for the interview. A few weeks later, I received a letter signed by the President of the Quorum of the Twelve Apostles, Ezra Taft Benson, calling me to be the Brazil North Region Public Relations Director for the Church. What an extraordinary demonstration of trust, I thought, for I had been a member for only two years and did not hold the priesthood. Yet I was to have the enormous responsibility of being spokesman for the Church in most of my country: the area included all the states of Brazil except for the lower four.

I immersed myself in this new opportunity, developing contacts in the newspaper, radio, and television industries. My position at Petrobras helped to open doors in the communications industry, and I was well received at large companies and major national television stations. The mission president invited me to participate in priesthood training meeting, where I talked about the importance of public communications. And I felt gratified each time positive articles about the Church appeared in newspapers and magazines. Somehow, the happiness that eluded me with every worldly success suddenly found a constant place within my soul as I strove for a higher purpose.

THE PRIESTHOOD

Even though Rudá and I knew all things would be restored in the last days, we felt that we would only receive the blessings that would come with my holding the priesthood in the millennium. Perhaps we believed the way we did as a defense mechanism, wanting to protect ourselves from any disappointments that false hope could entail. But for some reason, we never harbored expectations that any sort of change or revelation would occur during our mortal lives.

Still, we could not forget certain comments and observations fellow members would sometimes make. "Brother Martins," Heliton Lemos once said, "faithful members like you have demonstrated your claim on the priesthood to the Lord. I have no doubt that one day you will receive the priesthood." While we appreciated these demonstrations of goodwill and concern, we also consciously made an effort not to allow them to affect our lives as Latter-day Saints. We asked the Lord only for more faith, stronger testimonies, and the strength to serve.

São Paulo Temple, Brazil

©The Church of Jesus Christ of Latter-day Saints. Used by permission.

THE PRIESTHOOD

The Lord, however, had more in mind for us. In the years following our conversion and preceding that remarkable June day in 1978, when the prophet Spencer W. Kimball announced that all worthy male members of the Church could hold the priesthood, we experienced remarkable premonitory spiritual manifestations of what was to come. Still, we could not bring ourselves to even hope that the priesthood would soon be ours. In retrospect, of course, it is obvious the Lord used those years to prepare us for the revelation, even granting us encouragement from the prophet himself on several occasions. But we were slow to believe.

Strong spiritual promptings began for us in 1973, when Rudá, Marcus, and I received extraordinary patriarchal blessings—extraordinary because they promised blessings that, at the time, seemed impossible for our family to fulfill. The patriarch informed me that I would be privileged to live on the earth in the joy of an eternal covenant. Rudá received the same assurance. But how? How could we enjoy an eternal covenant when, as blacks, we could not go through the temple to be sealed?

Just as unusual was Marcus's blessing. In it, he was promised that he would preach the gospel to righteous families. Other parts of the blessing led us to believe he would serve a full-time mission. Again, how could this happen without the priesthood? We left the home of the patriarch confused, later deciding not to dwell too much on what had been said. We carefully tried not to let the promises in our blessings upset the tranquillity of our lives. Nevertheless, we couldn't ignore personal prophecy from God: we opened a mission savings account for Marcus Helvécio. Today, when I read my blessing, I shed tears at the significance and inspiration of the patriarch's words to my family that day.

Then, in 1975, spiritual experiences foreshadowing the priesthood revelation began occurring to us in earnest when President Spencer W. Kimball announced the construction of the São Paulo Temple. I was called to be a member of the public relations communications committee for the temple dedication and often attended meetings in São Paulo. One day, after one of these meetings, Rudá and I toured the construction site of the much anticipated temple, which we never expected to enter. As we walked on the uncompleted main floor, we both stopped at a certain place—a place which, we learned only later, was the very spot of the future celestial room. A powerful spirit touched our hearts as we stood there. We hugged each other and cried, not really understanding why.

Not knowing what to make of these unusual events, I simply went on with life, continuing to take care of my family, which grew to include two daughters, Marisa and Aline, and another son, Rafael. Meanwhile, my growing responsibilities with Petrobras included a significant amount of travel to all parts of Brazil. I always used my free time on these trips advantageously for Church public

THE PRIESTHOOD

relations. During this period, an article about the Church in Brazil appeared in the popular Brazilian magazine *Manchete*. It included a picture of stake presidents João Keminy and Valdemar Cury, mission president Hélio da Rocha Camargo, and me, mistakenly called a bishop. From that time on, everybody at Petrobras began calling me "Bishop." I tried to correct them, but they considered my denials a demonstration of humility. "We know you really are a bishop," they insisted so adamantly that eventually I stopped trying to convince them of their error.

In 1977, Rudá and I again met the prophet, President Spencer W. Kimball, who once again helped us to spiritually prepare for what was to come. On this particular occasion, the prophet had flown to São Paulo for the cornerstone-laying ceremony for the São Paulo Temple. He sat on a platform with his counselor President Marion G. Romney, Elder Faust, and other leaders. I was busily involved below with other members of the public relations committee. With the help of Douglas Borba of the Church's media company, Bonneville International, we assisted reporters from various newspapers, magazines, and television-radio stations.

Before the ceremony began, I glanced up at the stand and could see that President Kimball was looking in my direction. He motioned with his finger for me to come and speak to him. I turned away, not believing his gesture could be meant for me, and continued with my duties. Still, I couldn't help looking at him again. Smiling, the prophet repeated the signal, which I again could not believe was meant for me. Finally, he whispered something to Elder Faust, who then repeated the gesture and mouthed the words, "Helvécio, come here."

I excused myself from Brother Borba and went up to the stand. President Kimball stood up, gave me a hug, asked how I was doing, and introduced me to President Romney. Then the prophet put his arm around me, looked me straight in the eye, and said, "Brother Martins, what is necessary for you is fidelity. Remain faithful and you will enjoy all the blessings of the gospel."

I must have shown my confusion at this unusual counsel, because President Kimball obviously perceived my uneasiness. Believing I had not understood his words, he spoke to Elder Faust and, I think, asked him to explain the significance of this advice to me later.

I excused myself and left the stand, perplexed by the words of the prophet. Concentrating on my responsibilities proved difficult, but I tried to carry on. At the ceremony's end, President Kimball passed by the front of the line where I stood. He stopped when he reached me, took my hand with a strong grip, and, holding my arm with his other hand, told me, "Don't forget, Brother Martins, don't forget." Then he went on.

While I could never forgrt that encounter, its meaning became clearer to me only when Elder Faust presided over a stake conference in Rio de Janeiro months later. Before introducing Elder Faust as the last speaker, the

THE PRIESTHOOD

stake president requested that everyone in the audience remain seated so that our visitor could depart quickly to the airport for a flight to São Paulo. As the stake president spoke, Elder Faust handed a note to the stake executive secretary, who then brought it to me. "Could you please accompany me to the airport?" Elder Faust wanted to know. After the closing prayer, when Elder Faust walked into the congregation, I got up and left with him.

We took my car, and I drove quickly, thinking Elder Faust was late. "No," he said, "you don't need to go too fast. We have enough time." So I slowed down to enjoy Elder Faust's lively conversation. Before we reached the airport, he asked me if I remembered President Kimball's counsel. Had I correctly understood his words? I explained what I thought the prophet had told me and admitted that the experience perplexed me. Elder Faust then went on to explain that the Lord expected the same level of faith from everyone, even the prophet—thus I shouldn't think that the Lord expected greater faithfulness from me than from any of his other children. We all simply need to remain faithful, for only then do we have the right to God's blessings. "The promises of the Lord," Elder Faust told me, "will be fulfilled only in the lives of faithful servants."

I thought our conversation—very enlightening to me—had ended when we arrived at the Rio de Janeiro airport. As I drove to the curb to let Elder Faust out, he told me we had time to park the car. We entered the airport together and continued talking as we went into an unusually clean rest room. "It's a joy to enter places this clean," Elder Faust observed. "Our chapels should be this clean. Helvécio, if some day, you have the responsibility for the care and maintenance of a chapel, do all you can to ensure that it is clean and neat, so all will enjoy being there." Shortly afterward, the boarding call for Elder Faust's plane came over the airport speakers and we embraced one another. I returned home profoundly impressed with all I had heard and learned, and described to my family the unforgettable conversation I had shared with Elder Faust.

In 1978, my son's girlfriend, a very special young woman named Mirian Abelin Barbosa, returned from the São Paulo South Mission. Marcus had earlier experienced a spiritual confirmation that Mirian would be his wife, and they became engaged in February of that year. The marriage, they decided, would take place in May. Both families were happily preparing for the ceremony when the Lord intervened: Mirian decided to postpone the wedding.

She reasoned that, since Marcus did not hold the priesthood, her only opportunity to be sealed in the temple would consist of being sealed to her parents. Marcus and Mirian's marriage, consequently, needed to occur after the November dedication of the São Paulo Temple. Marcus agreed to the postponement. However, several months later, Mirian changed her mind. She and Marcus

THE PRIESTHOOD

set their wedding date for August 5, and the marriage preparations began in earnest. That brief postponement, from May to August, seemed insignificant at the time, but in retrospect, turned out to be profoundly important—an obvious example of the Lord's hand in our lives.

On June 8, 1978, I returned home from a typical day at work to find Rudá extremely excited. Two women were with her, one of them Yara Lúcia, the daughter of Rudá's friend Teresinha Bezerra dos Santos. "I have news, amazing news!" Rudá cried as I came through the door. "Rosana Wilken called Yara from the United States. The First Presidency just announced the prophet's revelation: the priesthood will now be given to all men, regardless of race! Helvécio, you will hold the priesthood."

I could not respond. Was it actually true? It couldn't be—we never expected it. Yet, would Yara and her friend come to our house with this news if it were not true? Still, I resisted believing this incredible report. Then our phone, which had been broken, suddenly rang. My associate from Bonneville International, Douglas Borba, told me from the other end, "I'm calling from Salt Lake City. The First Presidency just made the announcement about a priesthood revelation. I have the official declaration in my hands and I'm going to read it to you." He proceeded to read. My doubts disappeared. The foretold restoration had arrived.

I could not contain my emotions. Rudá and I went into our bedroom, knelt down, and prayed. We wept as we thanked our Father in Heaven for an event we had only dreamed about. The day had actually arrived, and in *our* mortal lives. Now, we understood President Kimball's admonition: "What is necessary for you is fidelity. Remain faithful and you will enjoy all the blessings of the gospel." Now we understood why Marcus's wedding had to be postponed: his patriarchal blessing promised him the opportunity to preach the gospel, an opportunity that would have been lost had he been married in May, just weeks earlier. Now we understood our own patriarchal blessings, promising us the joy of the eternal covenant in this life.

When Marcus arrived home from work, we told him the news. He quickly left for Petrópolis, the city near Rio where Mirian lived, to speak with her. The day, undoubtedly, was an amazing and very special one for us. From that moment on, our lives changed. While we did not receive the Aaronic Priesthood until two weeks later, immediately everyone wanted to talk to us, know our opinions, and hear our testimonies. Phone calls, letters, and messages poured into our home from fellow Saints.

One week after Marcus and I received the Aaronic Priesthood, we were ordained to the Melchizedek Priesthood. President João Eduardo Keminy of the Rio de Janeiro-Níteroi Stake ordained me an elder, after which I put my hands on the head of my son and, with the assistance of others in the circle, conferred the Melchizedek Priesthood on him. I felt I would explode

THE PRIESTHOOD

with joy, happiness, and contentment. What an incredible experience for me and for Marcus.

I began to have new opportunities in the Church and was soon called to be the stake executive secretary. Even more inspiring to me, experiences with the priesthood began occurring frequently, one after the other. It was as if the Lord accelerated my understanding of the priesthood's power. Until 1978, I had only been the beneficiary of the priesthood, and now the Lord was blessing me with countless experiences of being an agent of his power. Two particular experiences with the priesthood during this period remain particularly vivid in my mind.

The first occurred when Rudá called me at work one day, desperate because the young son of our maid, Maria José, had become deathly ill. I rushed home to find the boy cool and changing color to a light green. I anointed him with oil, placed my hands on his head, and in the blessing commanded him by the authority of the priesthood to come back to life. Even as I spoke, I could feel warmth infusing the boy's cold body, and when I opened my eyes, his normal color had replaced the green. The power of life returned, and this boy grew into a fine young man. Miracles happen; I knew that for a fact after that unforgettable experience, which was my first major experience as an instrument in the hands of the Lord.

The second experience took place when a woman in our stake called me one night, very upset about her husband. He was a good man, but suffered from emotional problems. On this night, he was particularly agitated, and had threatened to kill everyone in the house if his wife called a Church leader for help. "Brother Martins," she cried into the phone, "what should I do?" I asked her, "Sister, do you believe in the power of prayer?" When she said yes, I told her to hang up immediately and pray for help while I did the same. "Then, sister," I concluded, "do whatever the Spirit tells you to do."

After I hung up, I prayed and gave a blessing to this brother from my own home. In this blessing, I commanded him to calm down, get dressed, and go to the stake center where he could receive a blessing. I ended the blessing in the name of Jesus Christ and departed for the stake center, where I needed to attend auxiliary training meetings. As the meeting began, I saw this man and his wife enter the chapel. He was calm as they walked in and sat down on the back row. Humbly, I bowed my head and thanked my Father in Heaven for the privilege of holding the priesthood.

August approached, and so did Marcus and Mirian's wedding date. But Marcus's patriarchal blessing indicated he was to serve a full-time mission. When we discussed the situation as a family, Marcus's first reaction was, "What can I do? Practically all the marriage preparations have been made, and the invitations are in the mail!" I encouraged Marcus to talk to our stake president, João Keminy, which he did. President Keminy told Marcus to serve a mission. Marcus remained undecided.

Together he and Mirian prayed and fasted. Soon afterward, Marcus decided to go on a mission, and they once again postponed their wedding.

Before sending his mission application to Salt Lake City, Marcus made a special request on it: he wanted to be on his mission before his intended marriage date, August 5, 1978, only a few weeks away. With the help of the Church's executive administrator for Brazil, Elder William Grant Bangerter, the missionary department allowed Marcus to begin his mission before officially receiving the call. He went to the Brazil São Paulo North Mission and served under President Harry Maxwell, the former acting president of Ricks College. My son's faith in the gospel truly gratified me. As a result of his decision, the first three black missionaries to serve in the field came from three different countries: Jacques Jonassaint from Haiti, Mary Sturlaugson from the United States, and Marcus Helvécio Martins from Brazil.

TRIALS
AND BLESSINGS

The years that followed the priesthood revelation brought new opportunities to serve and a great deal of happiness to my family. At the same time, we also experienced tremendous challenges, including grave financial difficulties during the late 1970s. Finding the gospel and receiving the priesthood did not render my life worry-free. I think the Lord often prepares us for blessings by first letting us overcome trials. But even in times of difficulty, I continued to obey the Lord's commandments and, without a doubt, was repaid for my attempts to become, as Elder Faust admonished, a faithful servant.

Perhaps to prepare me for the blessing of holding the priesthood, the Lord first tested me and my young family. It all started in October of 1977, when I decided to retire from Petrobras. In Brazil, retirement benefits are based upon the number of years in the workforce, not upon a specific time with any one company. Because I had been working full-time since age twelve, I had more than enough years to qualify for benefits. Why not retire, I thought, and dedicate my time to Church public relations and teaching at the university? I did not hold the priesthood at the time, but I was willing to perform any service to help the Church, be it cleaning the chapel or maintaining the grounds.

Soon after I retired, a Church member approached me with a business offer. It was early in 1978. The proposal looked shaky, so I refused to become involved. The man kept insisting. I kept refusing. When I told Rudá of his idea, she also disapproved and encouraged me to stay away from the scheme. I resisted this member's persuasive efforts until he convinced me that the venture could help returned missionaries find work, often a difficult enterprise for young Brazilian elders and sisters returning from the field. So, against my better judgment—and without praying, fasting, or seeking inspiration from the Lord—I disregarded Rudá's advice and agreed to become a partner in the business. I put my savings into the business and allowed the company to use my name as a financial guarantor.

The business opened in April of 1978, two months before President Kimball announced his revelation about the priesthood. Several months later, in September or October, I became particularly busy with Church public relations, coordinating events for the public viewing of the São Paulo Temple before its dedication. I practically moved to São Paulo, staying as a guest in the home of a member and working most of the time at the temple.

During one of my rare stays at home, I was awakened one morning by someone insistently ringing my doorbell. I opened my door to find a police officer standing there with a court injunction requiring that I pay a large sum of money to the company's creditors. The company had failed, assuming many financial liabilities in the process. I signed the summons and the first of many difficult days began.

After I determined exactly what had caused the company's demise, I considered my options. As I pondered and contemplated the situation, my father's teachings about honesty and integrity, teachings I had tried to cultivate my entire life, along with the doctrines of the gospel, came into my mind. They convinced me that, because I had signed as the company's financial guarantor, I had to assume responsibility for the debts of even those who would not do their part. As it happened, the other partners indeed refused, or did not have the means, to fulfill their financial obligations. I would have to pay the entire enormous debt by myself.

We sold almost everything we owned, including our property in Rio and Petrópolis and our car, but still could not pay off the debt. At that point, I approached the creditors' lawyers and found one of them sensitive to my dilemma. Going against the wishes of his clients, this kind attorney worked out an agreement enabling me to pay at my ability and at a reasonable interest rate. Slowly, I began to pay off the debts.

Rudá, Marisa, Rafael, Aline, and I moved into a small rental apartment on Conde de Bonfim Street. But even living under tight financial constraints wasn't helping us progress: the money I earned from my pension and the university barely paid the monthly installment on the debt. How could we eat and live? I had three children at home and Marcus to support on a mission. Rudá, wonderful woman that she is, did not have enough experience to get a business job, so went door-to-door selling beauty products and manicuring nails. Marisa went with her, and thanks to them, we had enough money to care for our basic needs.

I prayed to Heavenly Father and pleaded with him to pardon me for the grave error I had committed. I needed his forgiveness and help. In confiding in the arm of flesh, I had not even consulted with the Lord, who could have kept me from making that disastrous business decision. I had also gone against my wife's counsel, and now innocent members of my family were suffering. How was I going to earn enough money to pay the debt and get our lives back in order? I began looking everywhere for extra work.

Our financial woes fortunately did not cloud our eternal perspective. I continued fulfilling my Church and temple responsibilities, and in November, my family and I partook of the spiritual feast of the São Paulo Temple dedication. Once again, we had the tremendous opportunity to speak with President Kimball, who approached Rudá and me at a press conference before the temple's dedication. Following his characteristic strong embrace, he asked me if I was happy and how I was feeling. How could I not be happy? Even the financial trials that had beset us couldn't dampen the joy of having the prophet of the Lord want to know if I was happy.

Our happiness, indeed, seemed complete when the São Paulo Temple, after eleven beautiful dedication ceremonies, opened one Monday for regular sessions. On November 6, 1978, my family joined Marcus, a missionary in São Paulo, and went through the temple together. The event prophesied in our patriarchal blessings five years earlier was finally coming to pass: Rudá, Marcus, and I received our endowments and our family was sealed together for time and all eternity by the first counselor in the temple presidency, José Benjamin Puerta. Marcus and Harry Eduardo Klein, then a temple worker, served as the witnesses as Rudá and I were sealed for eternity.

I will never forget the moment when, after Rudá and I were sealed together, our younger children, Marisa, Rafael, and Aline, came into the room and, together with Marcus, we knelt around the altar. The joy and gratitude of Rudá and Marcus, who understood the significance of the ceremony, shone in their eyes. Marisa, who did not yet fully appreciate what was happening,

TRIALS AND BLESSINGS

looked inquiring and observant. And little Rafael and Aline, who were too young to comprehend the importance of this step, simply expressed the wonder and surprise of happy children. For them, seeing us all in white was amusing. For us, it was overwhelmingly beautiful. A new beginning for our family had taken place, a major step toward exaltation in the highest degree of glory in the celestial kingdom.

Following the sealing, we still continued to live on the earth with its challenges and hurdles. Our financial troubles continued to daunt us. Yet Heavenly Father had heard my prayers, as always, and once again came to my relief. One afternoon as I was mulling over our problems, the phone rang. At the other end, the secretary to the vice president of Petrobras asked, "Doctor Martins?" in the Brazilian custom of addressing certain administrative levels and professions, with or without the academic title, as doctor. After I responded, she went on: "Doctor Artur would like to talk with you and wants to know if you could come in tomorrow." I immediately agreed to her request.

The next day I met with Dr. Artur. He asked me about my schedule and my work for the Church, to which I replied that, although I had been helping at the Church, I had free time available. "It is concerning that free time that I would like to talk to you," he responded and went on to explain that Petrobras needed a highly moral and responsible person to deal with a delicate project in one of their affiliated companies. "Because of your reputation in the company, your high moral principles, and your commitment to the Mormon church, you are the ideal man for this highly confidential position," he said. Petrobras had never before asked a retiree to come back, Dr. Artur explained, but the Board of Directors had approved my name, and the company needed me for about eight months of work

I could barely contain my joy at what this offer meant for me and my family. The salary Petrobras offered was very high. They would also give me a company car for personal use, replacing the one I had sold for the debt and done without. When Dr. Artur inquired, "When can you start?" I asked, "When do you want me to start?" His response was "Immediately."

The next week I began work as the director of administration and finances for the affiliated company, extremely grateful to the Lord for the opportunity to solve part of my problems. While the salary was large, even eight months of it would not be enough to pay off the debt completely. However, when I reported to the vice president six months later and told him I had finished the required work, he told me the company wanted me to stay on a little longer. That "little longer" turned into a total of eight-and-one-half years of work! Within that time, I received enough money to completely recover financially.

When Marcus Helvécio returned from his mission in 1980, our lives had returned to normal. Now debt free, we enjoyed even greater prosperity than we had before.

TRIALS AND BLESSINGS

These blessings greatly strengthened our commitment to the law of tithing, to service in the kingdom, and to the need to always go to the Lord before making important decisions. I was especially grateful that, throughout it all, I had been able to support my son on a mission. When he came home, Mirian was waiting for him. On December 19, 1980, Marcus and Mirian were sealed as husband and wife for time and all eternity in the São Paulo Temple, another powerful blessing for our family.

My bad business decision had taught me in a way I hoped never to forget that failing to seek or resisting the will and inspiration of the Lord can cause great pain. But during this time, conversely, I learned about the many ways in which listening to the Spirit brings great joy and allows us to carry out the purposes of the Lord.

In 1979, after having been called as a counselor in the stake presidency to President Antônio José Mendonça, news of my call reached the media. Stories about my call, inevitably focusing on my position as the first black to occupy a leadership position within the Church, had appeared in American papers such as the *Washington Post*. Brazilian journalists, in turn, learned about me through the U.S. publications and began to request interviews. Of these newspapers, the most important was *O Jornal do Brasil*. They sent a reporter, Cleusa Maria, and a photographer, Carlos Mesquita, to interview me at the stake center, and we stayed there for almost two hours. After we finished the interview, I offered to drive

Cleusa Maria and Carlos back to their office, and we enjoyed a pleasant conversation.

When I returned home that night, however, I became worried after reflecting on the preceding events. Cleusa Maria, I had noticed, took very few notes, and I could not see a tape recorder anywhere. Perhaps her purse contained one, but she never indicated the conversation was being taped. The more I thought about how she might portray the interview, the more concerned I became. Finally, I prayed and felt inspired to write a letter in which I clarified several key ideas in great detail, fearing that the article might not describe them correctly. Primarily, I wanted to leave a clear, distinct version of the points I made in the interview. Early the next morning, I went to the newspaper office and left the letter with the editor.

On Monday, January 22, 1979, "Helvécio Martins, Black High Priest: I Am Living Evidence that Racism Does Not Exist in the Mormon Church" appeared in print. Most of the article dealt with racism, and, to my pleasant surprise, quoted my words almost verbatim. The few minor details which were not entirely accurate in no way diminished the substance of the article. Surely, I thought, the journalist had taped the conversation. So, I started to wonder, why had I been inspired to write the letter? For a brief moment, I was perplexed—the letter seemed unnecessary. Then I went on to reason that perhaps the missive resolved things in the mind of the editor, and didn't worry more about it.

TRIALS AND BLESSINGS

Then, in early February, I opened *O Jornal do Brasil* and found my letter in the "Letters to the Editor" section. One other letter dealing with the article accompanied it, written by Antônio Lúcio from São Paulo, a prominent man who had visited two Brazilian presidents, Médici and Geisel, with the express purpose of speaking against the Church. His letter included several malicious accusations against the Church, and his assertions contradicted many aspects of my previously published interview. However, much to my great satisfaction and relief, the editor decided to print my letter, without contacting me, alongside his. My words amazingly touched on and answered every criticism Antônio Lúcio had made—it was as if I had actually responded to him before he even wrote his letter. How grateful I was for the inspiration that prompted me to write the response, as well as for the professionalism and honesty of *O Jornal do Brasil*. My letter must have profoundly silenced the accuser who, as far as I know, never again penned invectives against the Church.

My experiences in the stake presidency taught me a great deal as we worked to divide the stake. I quickly tried to cultivate in myself President Mendonça's competent leadership skills, one of the most effective of which was his powerful technique of delegation. We achieved our goal in May of 1979 when Elder David B. Haight came to Rio de Janeiro to preside over our stake's division. Called to serve as the first counselor of the new stake, I gladly accepted the counsel and advice Elder Haight offered

Elder and Sister David B. Haight, with Rudá and Helvécio, when Elder Haight set Helvécio apart as first counselor in the Rio de Janeiro Brazil Andaraí Stake.

throughout the weekend he stayed with us. He spent considerable time with me, and while his advice did not exactly tell me what would happen in the future, every point he mentioned prepared me for events to come.

The year 1979 continued to offer me amazing opportunities for enlightenment and growth. In October, I visited Church headquarters for the first time while attending General Conference—a trip that allowed me to learn more about Church history and see beloved friends. As the plane flew over Utah's mountain ranges, I contemplated the extraordinary treks of the early pioneers and the tremendous difficulties they encountered under those adverse conditions. Those feelings of reverence and respect for the pioneers returned to me as I walked on the sacred grounds of the Salt Lake Temple and thought of the sacrifices required to construct that building, raised in honor and homage to the Lord.

Waiting for me at the airport was the man who, many years ago, had come to my door as a nervous young elder: Thomas McIntire. A tearful reunion took place between us before I accompanied Tom and his wife, Marlene, back to their home in Kearns, where I stayed.

Attending the temple with these dear friends was a very special event. After the session, we met missionaries preparing to depart for various locations throughout the United States. One young man on his way to Philadelphia, who was certain he would be working with many people of my race, asked me what message I would send them.

I felt honored to give him my testimony, and asked him to write down my words to give to all he met during his mission.

Another particularly gratifying experience occurred after conference concluded, when Elder Bangerter invited Hélio da Rocha Camargo and me to his home for a family home evening. As Elder Bangerter drove us to his house in Alpine, Utah, he pointed out places he had worked as a boy. As we neared his house, I could see a flagpole with something hanging on it—from a distance it was hard to tell. When we came closer, I realized that a Brazilian flag flew from the mast. We felt honored not only by this welcoming gesture, but also by the displays inside the Bangerter home of souvenirs and mementos collected from Brazil during their various mission experiences there. After a friendly and warm meeting with the family, Elder Bangerter took us back to Tom's house, where I introduced everyone. Despite Elder Bangerter's many attempts to converse, Tom went red in the face and could not utter one word. Later, Tom explained that he felt so privileged to have a General Authority in his home, that he became totally speechless. I completely understood his feelings.

The following year Rudá accompanied me to October general conference. Again we had a wonderful experience, especially being in Salt Lake City during the sesquicentennial celebration of the restoration of the gospel. The highlight, however, occurred after the conference concluded. Elder Faust met with us in his office the following day and asked us, "Would you be available to meet with President Kimball tomorrow? He wants to talk with you." How could we not accept the invitation of the prophet? We immediately canceled our departing flight that afternoon to Sacramento and began a fast in order to have a receptive spirit for our meeting.

The next day, Elder Faust and Elder Ted E. Brewerton escorted Rudá and me to President Kimball's office. When the prophet heard our voices, he immediately came out to embrace us and invite us into his office. The next hour-and-a-quarter was filled with advice, support, warmth, and words of encouragement to resist the enticements of the devil. President Kimball also showed us around his office—telling the story of Heber C. Kimball, of whom he had a bust, pointing out mementos of various places he had visited, and describing worldwide locales with genuine familiarity.

The meeting, the interview, the combination of both, actually, was an incredible experience for us. The prophet made us feel as though he were just getting together with old friends. He literally emanated pure warmth and love. As we left, he walked us to the door, gave us an embrace and another kiss, and, holding my arm, said to Rudá and me, "I love you, brother. I love you, sister. Don't forget that I love you." With tears streaming down our faces, we left with an unshakable desire to testify of the sacred calling of a prophet. While our testimonies were not contingent on having personally met the prophet, they were certainly strengthened by looking into his eyes, feeling his magnificent spirit, and hearing his words. Even today, we can easily recall his powerful handshakes and embraces and our warm feelings during that meeting.

We visited with President Kimball on two other occasions, both in 1981, before his death. While his departure from this earth touched and grieved us, the prophet's death reminded us of mortality's claim on all of us. No one is granted an exemption from God's plan. We only regretted, however, that in all of our encounters with President Kimball, we never had a picture taken with him. Even though we sometimes had our camera, the prophet's unusual personality and powerful spirit so overwhelmed us that we always left him without remembering a photograph.

During this time, I continued serving as a counselor to the stake president. After two years together as a stake presidency, we began to pray for inspiration to replace the bishop of my home ward, Oscar Batista de Carvalho, who needed more time to attend to his son's special health needs. But weeks passed, along with countless discussions, and no name for a new bishop came to our minds. Finally, we decided to hold a special midweek fast about the matter. While fasting, I left to teach a class at the National Center for Technological Education of Rio de Janeiro (*Centro Federal de Educação*

Tecnológica do Rio de Janeiro). Before leaving the house, I prayed once again, asking Heavenly Father to help us discover the person he wanted to be the new bishop.

As I was driving quickly to work, already late, I entered Brasil Avenue, a large highway with heavy traffic. There, in my car, I received a personal revelation of who was to be the new bishop. It came to me much the same way a television screen's picture slowly appears just after the set has been switched on. And on the screen was me. *I* was to be the new bishop.

I mentally fought the idea. How could I, a counselor in the stake presidency, be released to be made a bishop? But the more I fought, the stronger and more vivid the image became in my mind. When I entered the classroom to teach, the image disappeared, only to reappear again after I finished the lecture. Finally, I resigned myself to the will of the Lord: I was to be the new bishop. After returning to my office, I locked the door, knelt, and thanked the Lord for his confidence, telling him I would do anything he wanted me to do. After my prayer, I calmed down and little by little quit thinking about the situation.

We did not bring up the subject the next week in presidency meeting, nor was it mentioned for several more weeks. Finally, a month later, when the stake presidency visited the Rio Comprido Ward, the stake president called me into the bishop's office. He opened his briefcase, took out a recommend for a new bishop, and, handing it to me, said, "Look." My name was on the form. When I told the stake president I had known for some time that I would be the new bishop, he wondered how I knew—he had not yet told anyone. On September 27, 1981, I was released from the stake presidency and ordained as bishop of the Tijuca Ward.

As bishop, I faced a whole new set of experiences, many of them difficult. From the beginning, many members of the ward resented having me, a relative newcomer to the Church, preside over them. They lived in a region where, decades earlier, the Church had gained a foothold in Rio de Janeiro. Several members had been baptized more than thirty years ago, had taken on many leadership positions, and were willing to serve. Why had the stake president offended the ward by calling a new member, already in the stake presidency, to become bishop? Changing feelings such as these required soul-searching, many interviews, and a lot of work to gain confidence, support, and help. But overcoming this challenge proved an invaluable learning experience, one which helped me grow as a leader and for which I remain grateful.

As always, though, the trials coexisted with blessings. I greatly enjoyed the daily experience a bishop has with the members in his ward. Particularly gratifying to me was helping new converts join the Church and less-active members return to our ward. One such case of reactivation particularly touched me and the other members

TRIALS AND BLESSINGS

involved. Sister Eunice Guigon de Araujo, one of the first members to join the Church in Rio de Janeiro back in the early 1940s, had worked as a journalist and successful radio actress at that time. However, after moving to Hollywood, California, she had a misunderstanding with her bishop which caused her to leave the Church and never return.

I heard about Sister Eunice, whose stage name was Susi Kirby, when I began working with Church Public Relations. Older members felt she might be able to help me publicize Church happenings in Brazil, recalling her radio and television roles, including a part in the soap opera (*novela*) "The Bones of the Baron" (*Os Ossos do Barão*). But Sister Eunice, or Susi Kirby, seemed to have magically disappeared. When I became bishop, I told the missionaries to keep their eyes out for this sister, and, sure enough, one day they found her.

I called the elders quorum president and together we went to Sister Eunice's apartment on Rademaker Street. After knocking at a half-open door without a response, we entered the apartment to find an elderly woman who had fallen on the floor. Completely disheveled, she shouted angrily, "Can't you see I've fallen! How dare you just walk into a house like this? Please leave and shut the door!" After we started to leave, a neighbor in the building went into Sister Eunice's apartment and then ran back out, explaining that this woman was sick and unable to stay on her feet, but was now up and willing to see us.

We again entered the apartment, this time to be greeted by the same older woman with uncombed gray hair and a wrinkled face showing the effects of time. When I introduced myself as a bishop of the Church, she began weeping and apologizing for the way she had treated us. She remembered the Church and had waited for this day, the opportunity to return. With some effort, she retrieved a small wooden box, from which she removed her baptismal certificate, perfectly preserved; photographs of her baptism in the ocean, where baptisms were performed in those days; and a picture of a birthday celebration. In that picture, missionaries surrounded a birthday cake Sister Eunice had made—a beautiful cake divided down the middle with an American flag on one side, a Brazilian flag on the other.

Gradually, Sister Eunice returned to full activity in the Church, beginning with home visits every Sunday afternoon from representatives from our bishopric, Relief Society, and Sunday School, and ending with attendance at all the Sunday meetings, including a temple preparation class. We had no idea when she would be called to the other side of the veil, and thus encouraged her to prepare for her endowment and then happily accompanied her to the São Paulo Temple. Fortunately, that day I brought along some of the old pictures Sister Eunice had shown me. When I showed them to Hal Johnson, the temple president at the time, he looked extremely surprised. Pointing to the picture of the birthday cake with the two flags, he cried, "Can you believe this? There I am in the middle of the picture. This woman made that cake to celebrate my birthday! Where is she? I need to see her now!"

A very touching moment followed when I led him to Sister Eunice. They immediately recognized each other and began crying, hugging, and speaking English and Portuguese simultaneously. President Johnson later came to Rio de Janeiro, where we reunited him with Sister Eunice again for dinner. It was the last time they were to see each other. Sister Eunice passed away in 1990.

Many memorable experiences such as these filled my tenure as bishop with incredible happiness and contentment. That calling, so shocking at the time I learned of it, enriched my life beyond belief. While I enjoyed my work in the stake presidency, nothing could match the day-to-day contact I had with fellow ward members as their bishop. Together we learned, progressed, and grew. I attended all my ward meetings with the exception of a Sunday spent celebrating my grandson's first birthday in Brasília. I was there for my ward and felt blessed by them.

In fact, after I had been a bishop for nearly six years—customarily, though not officially, the amount of time bishops normally served—I began to worry about my release. I loved my calling and the ward members so much that, during an interview with the stake president, I asked him to let me know several months in advance about my release. I needed to prepare myself psychologically for the experience. The stake president responded that he had not been thinking about releasing me. Still, I insisted that he let me know in advance when that day came. At the time, I did not realize that the Lord was already preparing my path to take a direction I never would have imagined.

FORTALEZA

The calling of bishop, and the way in which the Lord revealed it, had come as a great surprise. But I had no way of knowing that the late 1980s would bring an even greater and more unanticipated calling into my life. Like other opportunities to serve, this one would offer tremendous blessings, enriching my life and that of my family in myriad ways and helping us to grow spiritually like we never could have otherwise. Yet this new calling, with its unavoidable difficulties, involved a bitter challenge I had never before encountered—and hopefully will not deal with often in the future.

Before all of this happened, however, I was still happily serving as a bishop. In October of 1986, the missionary department in Salt Lake City contacted Rio Mission President Cory Bangerter, asking him to set up an appointment for me to visit with Elder M. Russell Ballard the following week. I could not imagine the purpose behind this meeting. When the day arrived, October 21, Rudá and I met with Elder Ballard, Elder Robert Backman (executive director of the missionary department at the time), and

Elder F. Burton Howard, the area president who served as translator. They asked us numerous questions, but kept the interview brief. Before Rudá and I left, Elder Ballard told us not to consider the meeting a calling, but simply an interview enabling the Church to assess leadership potential in the area.

Then, on the morning of November 3, I was working in my office when my secretary excitedly announced, "Doctor Helvécio, there is a phone call from the United States for you!" When I answered, President Gordon B. Hinckley of the First Presidency was on the line. "How are you doing?" he wanted to know. "Do you remember the interview with Elder Ballard?" Of course, I told him, after which he spoke words that took me by complete and utter surprise: "Your name has been submitted and approved. I am calling you, in the name of the prophet, to be a mission president." Caught completely off guard, I nevertheless replied that I felt honored and was ready to serve in any way.

When the letter I sent accepting the call became delayed in a Brazilian mail strike, Elder Charles Didier called me later in the month and I agreed that our conversation could be considered an official acceptance. He then authorized me to tell Church leaders who needed to know about my calling, but asked me to wait until the official announcement in the LDS *Church News* before letting others know. It was only then that I departed early from work to pick up my grandchildren at school and Mirian in Meier. I arrived home to Rudá and the children, then waited for Marcus to come over. After everyone was gathered together, I told them I had been called to be a mission president. Rudá cried as the rest of the room erupted with excitement. Rudá felt inadequate for that type of responsibility—as we all did. I think the Lord, however, calls us based on our potential and knew the Church would see to it that we left for a mission trained and qualified.

I was to serve as president of the Brazil Fortaleza Mission, newly formed from parts of the Recife and Brasília missions. One of the most important cities of Brazil's northeast, Fortaleza had, at the time, a population of approximately two and one-half million people. Since a branch had opened in Fortaleza in the late 1960s, the area had experienced significant growth in membership and development. A beautiful city, Fortaleza is renowned for its exquisite beaches.

Before leaving for the Mission Presidents' Training Seminar in Utah, I was released as bishop, an emotional experience that involved many tears—both mine and the ward members'. We had gone through a great deal together, but my new calling offered me the transitional support I needed. One month later, in May 1987, Rudá and I were on our way to the United States, where we received instruction from many qualified people, including several members of the Quorum of the Twelve and the First Presidency who made presentations. Among the mission presidents in our group was my good friend and former stake president Antônio José Mendonça, who had been called to preside over the Brazil, Recife Mission. We had been close since my conversion and continued to be so in our new mission responsibilities.

At the end of June, we returned to Rio de Janeiro. Then, accompanied by Marisa Helena, age twenty-three, Rafael, thirteen, and Aline, eleven, we went to Fortaleza to begin our new assignment. Waiting for us was LeRoy Drexler, the former president of the Recife mission, along with two assistants assigned to help us during those first weeks of our newly established mission. We found the help of those young men, Elders Fuzaro and Sanders, invaluable. As seasoned missionaries familiar with the city and with the other elders and sisters, they helped us to quickly familiarize ourselves with what was going on and what needed to be done.

We began by trying to get to know the missionaries and the local members. After meeting each missionary in an assigned zone, we would bear our testimony and express our desire to work with them to bring the gospel of Jesus Christ to that region of Brazil. The members, of course, numbered far too many to meet with individually, but we tried to work closely with them. When we began, Fortaleza had three stakes within its boundaries, and the cities of João Pessoa and Campina Grande each had a stake. Because missions are not responsible for stakes and wards, we only presided over several branches—in Mossoró, São Luis, and Teresina—and a full district in Belem.

Watching these branches, districts, and stakes grow gave me great satisfaction. The young men and women serving with us accomplished an extraordinary work in their new mission. The stake in Fortaleza gained almost enough new members for a division, while the outlying areas saw new branches and districts come into being, with potential stakes being planned in Belem, Teresina, and São Luis. Many good, committed people, including a current stake president, joined the Church in the area during our tenure, as we stressed not quantity of baptisms but quality of conversion. We wanted to bring true converts to Christ. The privilege of sealing in the temple many of the families who joined the Church in our mission has been a tremendous honor for me.

Another fulfilling part of being a mission president came from working side by side with Rudá in one of the few callings in which both the husband and wife work completely together. A mission president's wife, interestingly, is called and set apart as a full-time missionary and companion to her husband. She is at his side twenty-four hours a day. Rudá and I traveled together for hours by bus, car, and plane, going back and forth over the backlands (*sertão*) of Brazil's northeastern region to meet with the missionaries. We became much closer during those three years and learned many important things together: to communicate better with the Lord, to eliminate worldly things from our lives in order to become more spiritual, and to learn from people of all social, economic, and intellectual levels of society.

Most gratifying for Rudá and me as a couple presiding over a mission was the experience of becoming "parents" to 434 wonderful young men and women. A slight majority were Brazilians, most of the others Americans, but our missionaries' nationalities mattered little to us. We felt as though we shared fatherhood and motherhood with the parents of these dear elders and sisters, and we feel honored when they still write to us using the words father and mother. I often said to them that friendships, as well as families, are eternal. I like to imagine that, one day in the future, we will all gather in one large conference where we will worship the Lord and sing praises to our Savior and Redeemer as we did so many times in the Brazil Fortaleza Mission.

Serving our missionaries and helping them through their difficulties led us to seek the Lord more earnestly than we ever had before. Calluses actually formed on our knees from the many times during the day in which we would kneel and seek the Lord's inspiration. The phrase "President, I am telling you this because I trust you" often began letters from elders and sisters who shared their souls with us. I found helping them, praying for them, and serving as their bishop, stake president, father, older brother, friend, and confidante to be an immensely special responsibility.

President Martins with missionaries in the office of the Brazil Fortaleza Mission, 1989. From left, Elders Harris, Magerty, Mickessell, Franca, Ference, and Thirioty.

Our unique relationship with the missionaries initially brought up problems I felt unable to solve. The first time I read the following admission from a new missionary in his weekly letter, I didn't know how to respond: "I do not have a testimony. I thought that what I had was a testimony, but have recognized that it was actually the testimony of my father or mother. What am I doing here? I can't go to the home of Senhor Barros and teach something I do not believe. Maybe I should not be on this mission."

After asking this missionary to fast and pray with us and then come in to talk the next day, I passed along the counsel that the Lord had given me for him. He began implementing the suggestions. Gradually, he began to know for himself the truthfulness of the gospel, believe in the authenticity of the Book of Mormon, and gain a personal assurance that Jesus was the Christ. This type of experience occurred over and over with many of our missionaries, North Americans and Brazilians alike. With each transformation from doubt to faith and belief, we rejoiced, cried, and praised God for the miracle.

I never had the opportunity to serve a mission as a young man. Perhaps for this reason, I became particularly aware, as a mission president, of the invaluable preparation for all facets of life that a full-time mission can provide. In fact, I feel that the most important investment a family can make for the future of their children is to prepare them to serve a full-time mission.

FORTALEZA

It will enable them to develop a close relationship with the Lord, increase their testimonies, enlarge their intellectual abilities, expand their leadership capacities, teach them self-discipline, and let them experience the blessings of obedience. These and many other attributes return home with faithful missionaries, helping them go on to make great contributions to family, community, and society at large.

I was able to witness firsthand the development of worthwhile attributes not only in our missionaries, but also in our own family. Marcus Helvécio and Mirian, both returned missionaries, have enjoyed many happy years of marriage, in the process establishing a home for their three children which is pleasing to the Lord. Our second daughter, Marisa, who came to Fortaleza not particularly interested in missionary work, spontaneously and voluntarily began assuming missionary responsibilities. After filling a short-term mission, she went on to serve full-time in Brasília, and then she married Ricardo, a fine young man blessed with good values and a bright outlook for his future. While Marisa possesses many wonderful qualities, those that will help her the most in her marriage and throughout life she cultivated on her mission.

Our sojourn in Fortaleza, however, did not consist entirely of happiness and blessings. Missions are not missions without trials, and we expected that. But one difficulty in particular that we faced there shocked me. At no other time or place in my life have I felt the impact of racism as strongly as I did during our mission. It seems that, while was I prepared to deal with all types of people, some of my fellow Saints were not prepared to deal with me. Several times I was the direct target of racial hatred that greatly hindered the progress of missionary work in the area. At times, people concealed their racial prejudice, not openly declaring it, but letting me know their feelings through other, easily detectable ways. At other times, they manifested their claim to racial superiority clearly and obviously.

Before endeavoring to explain the roots of northeastern Brazilian race relations that clouded these members' perception, let me first offer my testimony as an authorized representative of the Church that The Church of Jesus Christ of Latter-day Saints is a racial democracy and could in no way be considered anything else. I have never, in any way, had any obstacle placed in my way by Church authorities due to any sense of racial order. The Lord testifies against racism in at least two places in the Doctrine and Covenants when he declares, "I am no respecter of persons" (D&C 1:35; see also D&C 38:16). And the Book of Mormon unequivocally lets the followers of the Lord know that "he denieth none that come unto him, black and white, bond and free, male and female ... all are alike unto God" (2 Ne. 26:33).

This is the word of God and this is his Church. What qualifies a person for the blessings and privileges of God's kingdom is not color of skin, size of bank account, or titles and degrees, but faithfulness to the principles, covenants, and laws of the kingdom. Because the glory of God is intelligence and the light of truth, those who dwell in the light of truth will be influenced by those principles. Unfortunately, those members of the Church who engage in racist thought and actions distance themselves from the light of the truth of the gospel. I have suffered from the consequences of their conduct. But I know that people are free to choose between good and evil, and the existence of a racist individual who is a member of the Church in no way makes the Church a racist institution.

The racism that affected some members in Fortaleza can be best understood in the context of the region's background and cultural traditions. In Brazil's early history, the northeast was considered the country's most important region. Cotton and sugar plantations that flourished during the sixteenth and seventeenth centuries provided abundant wealth for Brazil's mother country, Portugal. These crops necessitated the shipment of thousands of African slaves to work in the fields, slaves who went on to intermarry with Europeans and Indians. These marriages resulted in a significant majority of the northeast's population, particularly among the lower classes, being of mixed parentage. As a result, the wealthy elite did all they could to prevent racially mixed marriages from occurring within their families. The region consequently consists of a notable mixed or black population combined with a small white elite which has not intermarried.

Also contributing to racist attitudes in the northeast is the region's less-progressive economy, with its strong agricultural base. The high level of industrialization which has permeated much of southern Brazil has not greatly influenced the north, resulting in a socially conservative region which still clings to traditional beliefs about racial separation. I would even compare the attitude held by some of the northeastern elite to the attitude a century ago in North America and around the world: blacks have a prescribed role of subservience and innate inferiority. As a mission president and a well-educated businessman, I did not fit that stereotype. This bothered several local members when I came to Fortaleza.

One encounter particularly disturbed me. A male member from a prominent and educated family told me, face-to-face, that he detested blacks. Explaining that he could never accept me as a Church leader and mission president, he stated, "From the day you were called to preside over the Fortaleza Mission, a black cloud has hung over all of the Northeast." He also informed me that "as long as you are president of this mission, I will not return to church."

I was shocked by this unexpected and aggressive attack. Mustering enough self-control to mumble something to the effect that I felt sorry for him, I was nevertheless deeply disturbed and unable to react the way I should have, with more sincere goodwill and kindness. At the moment, my astonishment at this man's display of hatred prevented me from organizing my thoughts. The man realized this—that he had embarrassed and upset me—and left feeling victorious and profoundly pleased.

I returned home and went to the Lord in prayer, asking him to prepare me for future encounters with this man and, if necessary, others like him. Later, I visited this brother's home. He again treated me poorly, but this time I was able to turn the other cheek, telling him that, while I respected his right to disapprove of me, we should still try to follow our Savior's example of tolerance, goodwill, and meekness. It was because of such teachings of the Savior, I explained, that I had come to see him.

He responded by declaring that no matter how many times I repeated these things, I would not change his mind. I indicated that my purpose did not consist of trying to convince him. Our skins *were* different colors and we came from different races—circumstances well beyond our control. Despite these physical differences, we were both brothers in Christ, even though he might not like it. I sincerely hoped that in the future we could be together in the Church. As I left, he repeated his earlier assertion that as long as I was president of the Brazil Fortaleza Mission, he would not go to church.

He kept his promise. Not until I was released as mission president did this man return to activity. While he probably continues to harbor those same prejudicial feelings, I am grateful to say that my feelings for him are much more positive now than during our time together in Fortaleza—not because I am a superior person, but simply because the Lord changed my heart. In fact, I am even thankful for the experience because it prepared me for potentially more difficult encounters that may come. Now, I feel confident that, instead of becoming upset and losing my ability to respond, I will know exactly how to react.

Fortunately, such instances of racial intolerance were isolated occurrences in the northeast. Just as a prejudiced Latter-day Saint does not make the Church itself a racist institution, the existence of prejudiced Brazilians in no way condemns the country as a whole. My position in Petrobras required that I travel throughout Brazil. In my many travels—within the company, at the university, in conferences and symposiums throughout the country—I never experienced prejudice.

For this reason, it was interesting to me that, despite my age and extensive travels, a calling as mission president provided me with my first serious encounter with racial intolerance. I understand and accept what happened, and I do not blame anyone. I only regret that we lost opportunities to do an even better job because we lacked complete acceptance and support. I hope that someday these racist feelings will be eliminated. On that day, when the gospel produces this miracle, I will embrace everyone as my brother or sister in Christ.

Racial difficulties aside, most of the Saints in Fortaleza became wonderful friends whom we will never forget. Our last few months presiding over the mission proved emotional and trying. Leaving the close relationships we enjoyed with the missionaries, members, and people of the northeast seemed impossible. An extraordinary work had taken place and continued to go forth among the people of Fortaleza. Rudá and I, and our family, to this day, remain grateful to have been a part of it.

SERVANT OF THE LORD

I never imagined that I would be asked to assume positions of great responsibility within the Church. When I was baptized, of course, I did not expect to have the privilege of receiving the priesthood in my mortal life. Then, when I did receive it, I fully expected my Church service to continue on as it had, different than before only in that I now had the authority to give priesthood blessings.

However, my life as a Latter-day Saint developed far differently than the earlier scenarios I had envisioned. With each new leadership position, I became more humble and dependent upon the Lord, looking to him for help in carrying the responsibilities weighing upon my shoulders. My most recent calling has definitely carried more weight than any of the others, and, undoubtedly, came as the biggest surprise to Rudá and me. Only in knowing that the Lord had called me not because of my current qualifications, but because of what I could become, was I able to accept this responsibility.

As with my other experiences in leadership positions, this one began with an unexpected phone call. On the evening of March 23, 1990, my daughter Aline asked me to answer the telephone; from the static she could tell the call came from the United States. Because such calls came in almost routinely, I answered it without alarm. "President Martins?" inquired the voice at the other end. I answered affirmatively. "This is President Monson calling," replied the caller.

Immediately I thought it was a joke. My former missionaries now home in the United States often missed mission life in Brazil and called me. Often, they began the conversation with some type of joke—obviously what this introduction from "President Monson" was. So, always a good sport, I went along with the joke. Whether or not President Monson realized what was happening, he also went along with my peculiar responses until, at some point, he knew a mix-up in communication had occurred. "Is this really President Martins, President of the Brazil Fortaleza Mission?" he finally asked. "This is really President Monson, second counselor in the First Presidency. Do you know me?"

At that moment I realized my mistake and begged President Monson for his forgiveness. He accepted my apology and then went on to extend an invitation from the First Presidency to attend general conference in Salt Lake City this coming April, accompanied by Rudá. We were to leave the following Wednesday, go directly to our hotel upon arrival, and not go out too much. In taking these steps, he explained, we would avoid fueling speculation about why we were there by those who might recognize us.

After I told Rudá about President Monson's invitation and instructions, we wondered if this type of invitation to attend general conference could be a normal practice. When Rudá worried, I tried to distract her, suggesting that maybe we had done something so terribly wrong in Fortaleza that the First Presidency had called us to Salt Lake for a formal reprimand. This brought a laugh from Rudá. This little joke helped us maintain a semblance of control during the days of ambiguity leading up to our departure in late March. When we arrived at the Salt Lake Airport, we were met by an escort who took us to a hotel near Temple Square.

The day that followed was one of the most wonderful and difficult days of our lives. We nervously arrived at President Monson's office for an afternoon appointment. There, he graciously put us at ease—until he began the interview. During that meeting, President Monson told us something we never, never expected to hear: the prophet and First Presidency of the Church had called me to be a member of the Second Quorum of the Seventy, for the next five years.

All that Rudá and I could do was cry. I could not find any other words to say to President Monson except, "Why me?" I felt uneasy and unworthy. When President Monson asked whether I was willing to accept the call, I mentioned my inadequacies for this type of position. But I also remembered Nephi's declaration that the Lord does not give commands or calls without providing a way to complete the work. I believed in the Lord and humbly accepted the call. President Monson congratulated and embraced us, again counseling us to remain silent. So, we returned to our hotel and stayed there.

We then spent a restless night, trying to sleep without any success. At 6:30 in the morning, Elder Faust called. He knew how we must be feeling and invited us to his office to discuss the intimidating responsibility I had just accepted. There, he welcomed us, calmed us down, comforted us, and offered helpful counsel. Then, he called Elder L. Tom Perry, also of the Council of the Twelve, into his office and those two very special servants of the Lord gave us each a blessing. We gratefully returned to our hotel much more calm, composed, and able to control our emotions.

General conference began the next day. We continued following our instructions to remain discreet, but inadvertently ran into Elder Camargo, president of the Brazilian area at the time. "I don't know why you are here," he said, "but don't worry—I won't ask!" He and Sister Camargo then greeted us and went on without another word. We quickly found an inconspicuous place in the tabernacle for the first session.

During the second conference session, President Monson presented to the Church the names of the new

Elder Seigmiller greets Elder Martins outside the tabernacle on the day he was sustained to the Second Quorum of the Seventy.

©The Church of Jesus Christ of Latter-day Saints. First published in the *Ensign*, May 1990. Used by permission.

General Authorities. To hear my name presented, to be sustained, and to take my place on the stand with the other General Authorities greatly humbled me. How could I sit in one of those chairs, next to the men I admired so much? Often I had looked at pictures of them seated reverently during general conference and felt such great respect and love for them. To sit with them and number myself among them now was almost more than I could accept. But it was true. I sat down and looked into the congregation, relieved to see many Brazilian acquaintances whose expressions of love and kindness comforted and warmed my heart.

When the conference session ended, warm greetings awaited the new general authorities: Kenneth Johnson from England; Eduardo Ayala from Chile; and Harold G. Hillam, Lynn A. Mickelsen, LeGrand R. Curtis, Clinton L. Cutler, J. Ballard Washburn, Durrel A. Woolsey, and Robert K. Dellenbach from the United States. I first congratulated these good men before receiving a succession of embraces that seemed endless. I specifically remember Alfredo Heliton de Lemos, who had warmly welcomed us when we first visited that dilapidated church building in Rio. Brother and Sister Bangerter were there, too. Elder Siegmiller, one of our missionaries recently home from Fortaleza, heard my name announced at home on television, and was waiting at the tabernacle door to give me a strong embrace when I came out. How fortunate that I even have a photograph, taken and published by the *Ensign*, to remember that moment by.

Later, the new General Authorities were set apart, a moving and inspiring experience for all of us. President Monson ordained me a member of the Second Quorum of the Seventy. The first sensation I felt was one of complete exhaustion, followed by an awareness of my inadequacies. I also knew, however, that the Lord would compensate for what I lacked and help me to fulfill my new responsibilities. I humbly placed myself in his hands and still frequently review the counsel he gave me through Elder Monson's blessing, remembering the commitments and responsibilities I have been given.

The First Presidency informed us that we would finish the few remaining months of our mission in Fortaleza, then return to the United States with our family to wait for a specific assignment. Unbeknownst to us, our children already knew their lives would soon undergo tremendous changes. Word of my new calling had spread quickly in Brazil. When we called Marcus in Rio de Janeiro to share our news, he already knew about it. When we called Fortaleza, our children—Marisa, Rafael, Aline—and the missionaries also knew. Instead of hearing the news from me, they all heard it from our former Fortalezan missionaries, now home in the United States, who immediately called Brazil when they heard the announcement.

The fact that I became the first black General Authority for the Church received widespread publicity.

SERVANT OF THE LORD

Rudá and I found all the attention somewhat embarrassing, but felt that if the news helped others learn more about the gospel, we did not mind it.

Perhaps because of the media reports emphasizing my nationality and race, some members mistakenly went on to identify me as the "Brazilian General Authority" or as the representative for the black race in the councils of the Church. Whenever I have the opportunity to dispel this misperception, I do so, for I was not called by the Lord to represent any specific race, nationality, or ethnic group of his children. I was called by prophecy, revelation, and the laying on of hands to represent God's children—be they white, black, yellow, or any other color—wherever they live on earth. Evidently, it serves the Lord's purposes, *at this time,* for me to serve in the Brazil area presidency. But if, in the future, it serves the Lord's purposes for me to work with people in Asia, Europe, Africa, or anywhere else, I shall willingly go there.

Like Ammon and his brothers, I have a profound desire to declare salvation to all people, because I desire that not one soul should be lost. Humbly, I acknowledge my responsibility to represent the Lord and know that he is no respecter of persons. He does not consider skin pigmentation or race when awarding immortality and eternal life to his children, and that, he declares, "is [his] work and [his] glory" (Moses 1:39). As his servant, helping the Lord accomplish his work and his glory is my specific function.

Most members of the Church recognize that I, along with the other General Authorities, represent all people, and have been very supportive. During that unforgettable conference week, Rudá and I appreciated all of the well wishes from so many strangers we met. Much to our surprise, people on the streets of Salt Lake, Provo, everywhere we went—including the airport—stopped us to ask, "Aren't you the new General Authority from Brazil?" They would then hug and congratulate us, wishing us well in our new responsibility.

We spent a week in training and instruction before returning to Brazil, an immensely inspiring experience. During the week, the new General Authorities had the opportunity to bear their testimonies in a special temple meeting of the General Authorities in the area. When President Hinckley called my name, I did not think I had the strength to stand up. But as I stood in front of the prophets of God, the Spirit helped me to express the true feelings of my heart. I compared my beginnings in the Church with my experiences now, from the humble chapel on Joaquim Meia Street in Rio de Janeiro to the sacred temple room where we gathered. Before joining the Church, I had not been the worst person in the world, but the restored gospel of Jesus Christ had wrought tremendous changes in Helvécio Martins since he entered the gate of baptism leading to the kingdom of God. Meeting with the General Authorities in that temple room was something I never dreamed would happen, and I felt humbled by the experience. I asked for the brethren's help, understanding, and goodwill, and afterwards expressed my testimony and sat down. It proved to be a very spiritual moment for me.

We returned to Brazil and landed in Rio de Janeiro to go through customs and change planes. Marcus, Mirian, and our grandchildren—Flávio, Natalia, Filipe, and Ivete—were waiting for us there, along with Church members, relatives, and our nonmember friends. From there we flew on to Fortaleza, where time passed so quickly that, before we knew it, the end of June, and of our mission, had arrived. The new mission president, Atos Marques de Amorim, was a great friend of mine, often quipping that because we joined the Church within a few weeks of each other, we were "baptized in the same water." We greatly enjoyed introducing President Amorim and his marvelous wife to the Church leadership and missionaries in Fortaleza.

However, as much as we looked forward to our new assignment, we did not enjoy leaving Fortaleza and the many people we had grown to love there. When we left, the airport seemed too small to hold all of the friends who came to see us off. We did not want to bid farewell, and cried and cried as our plane took off for Rio. We stayed only a short time in Rio before going on to Salt Lake City, where we landed on July 24, 1990. After a brief visit with Elder Dean L. Larsen, a member of the presidency of the Seventy, we went to our hotel, where we stayed during a week of regular meetings with the Quorum of the Seventy. After that, we moved to the Mission Training Center in Provo, where my family took English classes.

A completely new set of experiences began for me at this point as I began accompanying members of the Quorum of the Twelve and the Seventy to various stake reorganizations. I learned a great deal from these powerful servants of the Lord and could feel the inspiration in their decisions, words, and the genuine humility they displayed. From Kembrook, British Columbia, with Elder Dallin H. Oaks; to Olympia, Washington, with Elder Neal A. Maxwell; to Mesa, Arizona, with President Howard W. Hunter; and to Morgan, Utah, with President Marion D. Hanks, I received an excellent spiritual education from these great brethren.

I also learned a great deal from the wonderful members we met and was truly surprised at the emotional reception they gave us during our conference visits. People literally emanated love for us—embracing us, sincerely offering gestures of kindness and friendship—no matter where we went. Even the Primary children greeted us so enthusiastically that, in the Morgan Primary, I could not hold back my tears at their warm welcome. Knowing that these devoted members displayed such honor and respect for us simply because we were representatives of the Lord humbled me. Everywhere I have traveled, I have seen and appreciated the love the Church members feel for the Lord and his gospel.

One of my most moving experiences to date as a General Authority took place during this training time in Utah when I was assigned to speak in the October 1990 general conference. Deeply aware of the many Saints my talk would reach worldwide, I sought the Lord's inspiration, receiving confirmation and reconfirmations that I should speak about the process new members undergo in joining the Church and gaining a testimony. I titled my talk "The Value of a Testimony."

I gratefully discovered I would be speaking in the second session, which would give me time to prepare emotionally for the moment. The extra time, however, in no way prepared me for the feelings that overcame me as the choir and congregation sang a hymn before my talk. I had planned to leave my seat and climb the stairs to the pulpit during the singing, but I became literally immobile with emotion and was unable to do so. With great effort, I finally freed myself from my chair, and began to climb a flight of stairs that seemed endless. As I reached the top, the brethren on the stand perceived my emotional state and all of them extended their hands in my direction, offering encouraging words. Their efforts helped me immensely, giving me the strength to walk to the pulpit and begin my talk.

I cannot describe what I felt as I faced the audience in the tabernacle that day. There I was, the son of Honório and Benedita, the husband of Rudá, the father of Marcus Helvécio, Marisa Helena, Rafael, and Aline, a recent member of the Church who less than thirteen years earlier had been given the priesthood. Now I stood at a pulpit that some of the greatest men of all time had occupied, with the living prophets and apostles seated directly behind me. Feeling humble and inadequate, I nevertheless felt privileged and blessed for this tremendous opportunity. Realizing again, as Nephi did, that the Lord will prepare a way for us to accomplish all that we are asked to do, I found the strength to continue speaking.

Fluency in the English language does not constitute one of my talents, but I believe that the Spirit and the gift of tongues enabled me to clearly convey my message that day. I testified that I know that my Redeemer lives and that I know that his Church is on the earth—the true Church of the Lamb of God, the Church of the prophets and apostles. I declared to all listening that the Book of Mormon contains the fulness of the gospel translated through the gift and power of God and that The Church of Jesus Christ of Latter-day Saints is the path by which we can return to our Father in Heaven.

After I declared these pure feelings of truth, the Spirit filled every fiber of my being and I felt the power and strength of the Lord warming my heart and clearing my mind so that I could give my prepared talk. As I concluded, a sensation of relief, peace, tranquillity, and serenity filled my soul. I walked back down the stairs, found my chair, sat down, and wept.

I returned to my native country as a member of the Brazil area presidency, serving with President Joe J. Christensen and Elder Harold G. Hillam. Working with these men has been a great privilege, and as we have served together, my confidence in the Lord and understanding of his Church has grown. Area presidencies are responsible for certain programs, and all stake, mission, and regional leaders report directly to us. We also serve as a governing council for the area and discuss all decisions and actions pertaining to the Church in Brazil in our meetings.

I wanted nothing—either spiritual or physical—to impede my contributions as a General Authority and the increased amount of work and travel it entailed. With that in mind, in November of 1990, I went in for a physical examination at the Albert Einstein Hospital in São Paulo. I specifically wanted an evaluation of my spinal column's condition, since several years after my automobile accident, doctors discovered one small fracture in my neck that, unlike the rest of my body, had not properly healed. Since the discovery of the fracture, I had continued in good health, but wanted to know if the problem could eventually be debilitating and interfere with my work.

Unfortunately, Dr. Murachovisk's answer was yes. The fracture would continue to separate with age and deteriorate with time. I would feel increased discomfort and experience reduced physical capacity. What's more, he warned, if I were not careful, avoiding even such moderately physical activity as skipping steps while climbing or descending stairs, a resulting lesion of the cord could prove fatal. Because of the risks involved, corrective surgery was not advisable. I would simply have to live with the problem.

I continued on with my life and its routines after that, mildly apprehensive about my health possibly taking a turn for the worse. Then, in mid-July the following year, 1991, after completing some sealings in the sweet, spiritual atmosphere in the house of the Lord, I began to contemplate my existence. I remember thinking that, while I did not know how many days I had left in this world, I hoped that the rest of them could be as profitable as possible. As I left the temple and hurried to my office, where I had people waiting, the same thoughts returned to my mind: I wanted to do and serve all that I could for the rest of my life, without any circumstance robbing me of my physical abilities.

Still deep in thought, I went against the recommendations of my doctors and ran down the stairs separating the temple grounds from the parking lot. Nothing happened, but a peculiar insight crossed my mind. I envisioned falling and wondered whether the strong jolt of a fall could miraculously knock my back bone into place. "Wouldn't that be a blessing?" I thought to myself. "I would not have to worry about my future health." My thoughts then turned to genuine supplication to the

Lord as I sincerely asked him to help me overcome this physical problem.

The next morning, I woke up as usual at 5:30 and went into the bathroom. After showering and dressing, I started to return to the bedroom, but both of my feet slipped on a rug and I fell backwards. I hit the back of my neck on the sink, receiving such a violent blow that I thought I had died. I could not speak and had the impression that my body was floating in the air. "Has my body died and my spirit doesn't realize it?" I wondered. With all the force I could muster, I tried to call out to Rudá. Not a sound came out. Then, because I thought I was probably not living in this world, I called with all of my strength to Heavenly Father. Rudá did hear that cry and ran in to see what was wrong.

Frightened at my state, Rudá woke up Rafael and Aline to come and help. I quickly told them to find my address book, which I had providentially brought home from work the day before, not knowing why. I instructed them to call the Albert Einstein Hospital phone number, and explained what they should do at the hospital and with my checkbook, taxes, and documents. I also asked Rafael, sixteen at the time, to come close to me for some advice I did not want him to forget.

The ambulance quickly arrived and took me to the hospital, where Dr. Murachovisk ordered an X-ray of my head, neck, and back. He could not believe the fall hadn't killed me. Instead, the opposite had occurred.

The fall not only avoided injuring any part of my head or neck, but also incredibly eliminated my fracture problem from my old injury! All my vertebrae now lined up in their correct places and could be safely secured in place with surgery. The doctors were astounded.

When Rudá and Dr. Murachovisk came in to tell me the news of my spine's condition and the need for surgery, they were surprised at the big smile on my face. I told them what had happened the day before at the temple and declared that this accident was a clear, indisputable answer from the Lord to my fervent supplication. On July 19, 1991, Dr. Reinaldo André Brandt performed successful surgery on my back, an operation that lasted for four and a half hours.

Before, during, and after surgery, angelic beings personally ministered to me. One of them was my mother, who had passed away in 1964. I was talking to Rudá and the hospital room filled with my mother's presence. She was there. I could see her pleasant face, without wrinkles. Her hair was completely black and her eyes had that loving glow I remembered as a child, transmitting peace, tranquillity, and confidence. I cried the entire time my mother was with me, although I have no way of knowing how long the experience lasted—possibly only two or three minutes, but it felt like a long time.

Ten days after the operation I returned home wearing a body brace to immobilize my backbone and make certain everything mended properly. The doctors had no precedent case to refer to, but estimated that I would require the brace for at least sixty days, maybe longer. It was during this period of physical incapacity that I dictated most of this, my story, hoping that my modest history could help members of the Church who are struggling, as I do, with life's problems.

Little by little, I began to resume my responsibilities in the area presidency. One month after surgery, I began going to the office for part of the day, spending the rest of it in physical therapy. While the brace, to me, represented an instrument of medieval torture—uncomfortably rubbing on both sides of my head, chest, stomach, back, and shoulders—I felt good spiritually. The discomfort caused by the brace, after all, seemed an insignificant price to pay for the blessings I had received.

The Lord gave me the complete physical capacity and potential I had requested. I now have the ability to serve him as I so greatly desired. God was, and continues to be, a God of miracles. He is the same yesterday, today, and forever (see 1 Ne. 9:5–6; 2 Ne. 27:23; John 15:7). People's disbelief, impatience, dishonesty, and lack of sincere purpose often prevent miracles and blessings from occurring in their lives. But I proclaim my testimony that the Lord can and does perform miracles, and I am profoundly grateful for the one which enabled me to continue my duties as his servant.

EPILOGUE

It is now four years since my calling as a General Authority, and I still harbor strong feelings of inadequacy. These insecure feelings, however, are tempered by faith in the Lord. Knowing that he qualifies those whom he calls encourages me to continue striving and going forward, for in the kingdom of God, nothing is static. We are all progressing as part of the plan, hopefully fulfilling the will of God in our efforts to move ahead.

Many years ago, after organizing the first stake in Rio de Janeiro, Elder Bruce R. McConkie gave the new leaders some advice I found inspiring and insightful. They worried because of their lack of experience and dependence upon a manual to learn to run a stake. Elder McConkie compared their situation to that of a train engineer traveling on a dark night to a place he had never been before. The only light in the blackness came from the engine, and it only illuminated the first hundred yards in front of the train. But as long as the engineer kept the train moving, concluded Elder McConkie, that small light would project ahead so that he could always see where he was going.

The Martins family: (back row) Raphael, Aline, Marisa Helena, Flavio, Miriam; (front row) Filipe, Helvécio, Rudá, Marcus Helvécio, and Natalia.

To this day, I consider that analogy to be very instructive. Whether we are called to serve as a Sunday School teacher or a priesthood leader, once we receive the authority to act in that position and strive to comply with the Lord's will, he will provide enough light and assistance for us to do our part. We may not completely understand our responsibility, but the Lord will provide enough knowledge to accomplish the immediate needs of our task. Then, as we progress, we receive more help. Helping us along the way are the scriptures, inspiration through fasting and prayer, and Church manuals for instruction.

The Lord will be able to perform miracles and great works through us if we live the commandments, develop Christlike attributes, and have faith that he will help us overcome weaknesses. Conversely, we can slow down the Lord's work with our lack of faith, which renders us fearful and hesitant to carry out the Lord's will. The disciples feared greatly when their boat tossed amidst the powerful waves of the sea and began to fill with water. "Master, carest thou not that we perish?" they cried to the sleeping Savior. Jesus then calmed the waves and rebuked the storm, saying, "Peace, be still." Afterwards, he turned to his disciples, asking them, "Why are ye so fearful? how is it that ye have no faith?" (Mark 4:38–40). He knew that fear stems from a lack of faith. Those with faith do not cower and waver, but confidently move forward, trusting in God.

EPILOGUE

I also believe the word *impossible* is used by people of limited faith, for the Lord knows our capacities and knows we can do more, with his help, than we think we can. When we resign ourselves to the fact that we did not complete an assignment, but instead did only what we could "possibly" do, our responsibility went unfulfilled. The Lord, however, knows that with him all things *are* possible, for we are gods in embryo, capable of growing from grace to grace. With faith and effort, we can reach heights we would otherwise consider unobtainable.

In my own life, I found that as I cultivated this principle of faith and effort, I went from a position of privileged spectator to that of legitimate builder of the kingdom. Making this leap has brought me so much happiness that at times I feel my soul will explode with joy. That the Lord guides and inspires our work in the Church and that we serve as his instruments is an overwhelming realization, for we need to prepare and ready ourselves for his constant use. This is the challenge for those who serve, to become instruments in the Lord's hand. This is my challenge, and I plead with him that I can always do what he desires, regardless of what it may be, that I might become this type of magnificent instrument.